LE

LEFT AT

THE PASTRYCOOK'S:

BEING THE CLANDESTINE CORRESPONDENCE

BETWEEN

KITTY CLOVER AT SCHOOL

AND

HER "DEAR, DEAR FRIEND" IN TOWN.

EDITED BY

HORACE MAYHEW.

ILLUSTRATED BY PHIZ.

LONDON:
INGRAM, COOKE, AND CO., 227, STRAND.
1853.

LETTERS LEFT AT THE PASTRYCOOK'S.

MR. PENN, THE WRITING MASTER. (*See page 44.*)

CONTENTS.

LETTERS

LEFT AT THE PASTRYCOOK'S.

THE accompanying Letters were rescued from the butter-shop in the most miraculous manner. I had been waiting for some time at a fashionable pastrycook's—which was then in Tottenham-court-road—to keep a business appointment. I had read every ginger-beer and soda-water label round the room. I had admired all the different varieties of architecture and bird-cages, to which barley-sugar lends its glittering but fragile aid. I had carefully noted down on the porcelain tablets of my recollection the many fanciful forms of zoology, into which sponge-cake, like a second Proteus, delights to metamorphose itself. I had watched, with a feeling of envy and tender regret that I couldn't do the same, the little children playing with their Bath buns, first picking out the white plums, which, like pearls, adorned the coronet of their sugary brows, and then slowly eating the bun in small pieces, as if to make the most

B

of a pleasure which they were conscious was too sweet to last
for ever. I had imbibed glass after glass of cherry-brandy,
until I felt as if another cherry would have choked me ; in
short, my patience, my admiration, and my appetite were alike
exhausted, and I was registering a vow in that mental office in
which indignation sits frowning to receive the vows of lovers,
patriots, and all injured persons, never to transact any more
business at a pastrycook's shop, when the postman entered, and
demanded " tuppence" for an unpaid letter, which he had flung
down upon the counter. The young lady standing behind it,
with the pretty lace cap that looked so light and frothy, that
one's imagination, kindled by the locality, pictured it as having
been spun out of a dish of trifle, examined the letter, and, in
a sharp tone, which cut short all remonstrance, said, " I shall
not take it in." She then pulled down from the shelf a little
bundle, black with long neglect, which was lying on an empty
box of kisses, and displaying them, like a pack of cards, said,
" I have already got all these—not one of them has been fetched
away, and I'm determined to take in no more. These I shall
sell to-morrow for waste paper." Luckily I had twopence still
left after my reckless extravagance of cherry-brandy, and I
requested the young lady, in so many words, " to be kind
enough to allow me to pay the twopence, and, further, to increase the obligation, by adding the letter, which had so narrowly
escaped being thrown upon the wide world, to its little lot of
orphan companions." These two requests she smilingly com-
plied with ; and, a month afterwards, the letters still being in
durance vile, she was not proof against the temptation of a
large sum of money, which my curiosity, backed by a strong
feeling of sympathy, prompted me to give, to release them from
their dusty captivity. I should have been well repaid for this

outlay by the interest of the letters themselves ; but I am bound
in justice to state that their ransom money, as well as the
twopence originally expended, have been refunded to me since
by my liberal publishers, Messrs. Ingram & Cooke. On examination I found there were no names to the correspondence
beyond those of "Kitty" and "Nelly," which, being pretty
names, I have retained ; neither was there any address inside
the letters, nor any clue, indeed, by which I could trace out the
fair heroines of them. The other names have either been added,
or altered by myself. Under the circumstances, therefore, I
hope there is no harm in my publishing a correspondence I came
so curiously in possession of. I know nothing whatever of the
"Princesses' College," or of the persons whose Christian
names are mentioned in it ; and, having fairly purchased the
letters, surely I have a right to do what I please with them,
more especially when no one is likely to be injured or compro-
mised by the innocent result.

One plea more, and I have done. The object of the letters
having been written was, as I imagine, to be read by the person
to whom they were directed. It is as clear as isinglass, therefore, that there is more chance of this object being fulfilled by
the letters being circulated far and wide in the drawing-rooms
of the civilised world, than in their lying with the inscription
"to be left till called for," carried out most mockingly to the
very letter, unopened on a dusty shelf at a pastrycook's shop
in Tottenham-court-road.

With this explanation, I leave "Kitty's Letters" to speak
for themselves. The originals are left with the publisher, at
the office No. 227, Strand, in case Kitty, or Nelly, should feel
inclined to call and claim them in person.

THE FIRST LETTER LEFT.

(Dated February 10th.)

SHOWING HOW KITTY WAS TAKEN TO SCHOOL BY HER "WICKED MAMMA."

OH! my darling Eleanor, it is all over!—and yet I live; but I have strong hopes of dying before to-morrow morning. I feel that I can never exist within these hateful walls, to be a wretched slave to Mrs. Rodwell's "maternal solicitude and intellectual culture." What do I want with intellectual culture indeed? But I'm determined I won't learn a bit—not a tinny-tiny bit!

I must tell you, dearest, that before leaving home I cried continually for at least three weeks; but my tears made not the slightest impression on mamma's hard heart, which, I am sure must be stone. More than this, I starved myself during the last three days—did not take one luncheon—even refused pudding; and at Mrs. St. Vitus's ball would not dance, nor touch a thing at supper. But all in vain! No one seemed to care a pin about it; and Ma only appeared to take pleasure in my sufferings. The boys teased, and made cruel jokes upon my misery; and that detestable Martha helped to get me ready as cheerfully as if I—no, *she*—was going to be married. The last day I went into hysterics; and looked so ill—with my red eyes and pale cheeks—that Ma, to my great joy got frightened, and sent for Dr. Leech. But that cross old monster only dangled his bunch of big seals, and said that I should be better at Turnham-green—a little change of air would do me good! Much he knows about medicine; for at the very moment he was talking, I felt as if I must have fainted.

So in a cold drizzling rain—will you believe it, Nelly?—I

was dragged into the carriage (for Pa had walked down to the office on foot, carrying his own blue bag, purposely that Ma might have the carriage), and propped up on each side with bags of oranges, cakes, and goodies, to cheat me into the stupid notion, I really imagine, that I was going to have a treat, in the same way that nurse always gives Julius his powders, with lots of sugar on the top! Oh! my sweetest Eleanor, words cannot express the wretchedness of your poor friend during that long ride! And yet Oates never did drive so quickly; he seemed to be doing it on purpose—whipping the poor horse through Hyde-Park as furiously as if we were trying to catch a mail-train, instead of going at that delicious crawling pace which we have always been accustomed to by the side of the Serpentine. Opposite Lord Holland's Park the horse fell. Oh, how my heart beat to be sure! I thought he was killed at least, and that we should be obliged to return home; but no such thing. He picked himself up as quietly as you would a pin, and the carriage went on even faster than before.

But after all, Eleanor, what pained me most was mamma's and Martha's cold-hearted conversation whilst I was in a corner suffering so much! They chatted as cheerfully upon worldly nonsense as if we were going to a pantomime. I shall never forget their cutting cruelty at such a moment as that; and, to make matters worse, what with crying and the rain, I felt as wet through as if I had been travelling along the submarine telegraph, besides *my tears spoiling my pretty puce-coloured bonnet strings which were new that day.*

At last we stopped before a large, cold-looking house, with walls pulled tight round it, like the curtains of the four-poster when Pa's ill in bed. It was all windows, with bars here and there, and the plaster looked damp, and, altogether, it was much more like a convent than a College; for I must tell you our school isn't called a "school" (for it seems there are no schools for young ladies now-a-days), nor a "seminary," nor an "academy," but it's a "College." I thought I should

have fainted away, only I had the cakes and oranges in my
arms, and was afraid of dropping them down the area, when
Mrs. Rodwell took me upon her "maternal" knee, and began
stroking me down and calling me her "dear young friend,"
with whom she said "she should soon be on excellent terms"
(only I am sure we never shall, excepting the "excellent terms"
Pa pays her), and she went on playing with me, Nelly, just
as I have seen the great big boa-constrictor, at the Zoological
Gardens, cuddle and play with the poor little rabbit, before he
devours it.

And now, dearest, mind you never mention what I am going
to tell you ; but all the sentiment and fine talking and writing
about a mother's love is nonsense! utter nonsense! all a de-
lightful sham !—for all the world, Nelly, like those delicious
sweet *méringues* at the pastrycook's, which look like a feast,
and only melt into a mouthful! I am sure of it, Nelly dear, or
else how could they bear to make us so miserable? looking
quite happy whilst our poor hearts are breaking? sending us
from our natural homes, where we are so comfortable, to such
miserable places as this "Princess' College!" and especially,
too, when governesses now-a-days are so plentiful, and far
cheaper, I am told, than maids of all work! Why, it was only
last Friday morning I showed Ma the most beautiful advertise-
ment there was in the *Morning Post*, all about a governess
offering to "teach English, French, German, Italian, Latin,
the use of globes, dancing, *and crochet-work too*, and drawing,
painting, music, singing, together with the art of making wax-
flowers actually, and all for 21*l.* a year!" But Ma only
patted me, and said she "should be ashamed to encourage
such a terrible state of things," or some such stupid stuff that
put me in a passion to listen to. I am sure I shall never believe
Ma loves me again, after throwing me from her dear fat
arms into the long thin claws of that awful Mrs. Rodwell!
They opened and shut, and closed round me, Nell, exactly
like a lobster's !

FIRST INTRODUCTION TO THE SCHOOLMISTRESS.

(See page 7.)

Before I could escape, Ma and Martha were gone, and I was left alone—all alone—in this large dungeon of a place, with every door fast. Well, Nelly, you have been to school—at least I suppose you have—so you can imagine how I was allowed to remain in the schoolmistress'—no, our schoolmistress is called a "Lady Principal"—in the Lady Principal's *boudoir* to compose myself; how I was treated to weak tea and thin bread and butter with Mrs. R., and asked all the time all manner of questions that made my cheeks burn with rage, about home, and about mamma and papa, until eight o'clock came, and with it the permission to retire, as "bed would do my head good." I was too glad to get released, if it was merely to indulge my grief, and cry myself to sleep underneath the bedclothes!

But, law! if it was so uncomfortable in the *boudoir* (and such a *boudoir*, Nell!—a dark closet with a handfull of cinders for fire, and full of gimcracks, little pincushions, lavender baskets, painted card-racks, and fire-screens, until it seemed furnished from a fancy fair)—but if that was uncomfortable, I say, it was positively wretched in the bedroom; with its six iron cramp-beds, three washing-basins, and one looking-glass! Yes, Nelly, only one looking-glass amongst six young ladies! I never heard of such a thing. And then the place was so, *so* very cold, that I am sure I shall have a red nose and chilblains for the remainder of my life; *but I hope, my dear, fond Nelly, you will love me all the same!*

Well, I cried myself to sleep, and it was a great comfort, I can assure you; and it seemed still in the middle of the night, when a loud ringing in my ears frightened me out of my sleep, and made me nearly fall out of bed. And, after that came a sharp, barking voice, calling out, "Now, young ladies! are you going to breakfast in bed?" and causing a general stretching, scuffling, and jumping up.

The cold glimmering dawn lighted only portions of the room, but I could see five other girls creeping about, half asleep, quarrelling for basins, engaging turns at the *one* looking-glass, joking, grumbling, yawning, and laughing; whilst I, poor I, sat hope-forlorn, shivering, half with cold and half with fear, on the edge of the bed. There a tall young lady, in a flannel dressing-gown, discovered me, and exclaimed, "Why, here's the New Girl! I say, my young lady, you had better make haste; the second bell will soon ring, and Miss Snapp will give you something to cry for if you're not ready."

Then they all came and stared at me (the rude things); and as I could not help crying, one of them called out, "Oh! Oh! how affecting! Oh! Oh! *Oh!* OH!" ending at last in a loud bellow, in which I joined in painful earnest; and then they left me, and went on whispering, washing, combing, and lacing each other, until "Ding, ding, ding," went the second bell; and at the first sound they all scampered away, some with their dresses still unfastened, calling after others to come and hook them for them.

I never should have got finished myself, unless a mild, quiet-looking woman had ventured to my assistance, and led me down stairs into the school-room, where I nearly dropped upon *feeling* the stare of some fifty girls fall upon me all in a lump, just like the water from a shower-bath after you have pulled the string. Oh, darling Nelly! what would I have given for one familiar face that I knew, or to have had your loving self by my side, so that I might have thrown my arms around your dear neck, and have a *good cry;* for I am sure that a good cry does one, frequently, much more good than a good laugh!

The buzzing, which had suddenly ceased on my appearance, began again with double vehemence, making nearly as much noise as the water, when it's running into the cistern at home. Amidst the hurried whispers, I could detect, "What a milk-sop!" "Mammy's darling!" "She'll soon be broken in!" &c.; when the same dog-like voice was heard to bark again, calling out above the uproar, "To your seats, young ladies! Silence! Five forfeits for the first who speaks!"

In the lull which followed, I was seated by the side of my quiet conductress, and permitted to write this letter to my dear darling Eleanor, just to fill up my time before breakfast, after which I am to be examined and classed according to what I know.

Oh, Nelly, I do so dread this day, and am so extremely wretched, thinking all the time what they are doing at home, and how Martha is rejoicing that she has got her sister away from home. But I must leave off, dearest ; and I will promise you several more letters (that is, of course, if I survive this day), in which I will tell you of everything that occurs in this filthy school—I mean College. That will be the only ray of pleasure, Nelly, which will shoot in this dark dungeon through the captive heart of your devoted, but wretchedly unhappy

Kitty Clover.

P.S.—Excuse haste and my dreadful scrawl.

P.S.—You will see I have forwarded this to the pastrycook's in Tottenham-court-road. Do not eat too many pink tarts, dear, when you call for it.

P.S.—We hear a great deal, Nelly, about the trials and troubles of the world, and of all we have to go through, and about school being the happiest time of our lives ; but they seem to do all they can to make it miserable, and I don't believe any hardship on this world is worse than going to school, and having to face fifty girls, all making fun of the New Pupil.

THE SECOND LETTER LEFT.

(Dated February 14th.)

SHOWING HOW KITTY FARED (OR SCARCELY FARED AT ALL)
THE FIRST DAY AT SCHOOL, AND THE DREADFUL DISASTER
THAT BEFEL HER.

OH! my dear Nelly, I'm in such a mess, and can't think
how I am to get out of it. I would run away, only I don't
know where to run to: and, besides, all the doors are fast;
and more than that, I feel Ma would only bring me back again
if I were to get away. Only think of that mean Mrs. ——
(you know who I mean) opening all the letters; and I never
knew this until my letter was in her bag. Miss Sharpe (who
has promised to give this to some one who will drop it in the
post on the sly for me) says every word we write home, and
every word we receive from home, is pried into, and very often
kept back if it does not exactly please the Lady Principal! A
pretty lady! I wonder she isn't ashamed of herself! A nice
example to set us young girls—actually teaching us to go a
peeping into other person's secrets! Meggy (that's Miss
Sharpe's name) says she intends speaking to her papa about it.
He is a Scotch lawyer; and she has often heard him say that
there's a fine of 100*l.* for any one who breaks a seal upon trust
papers! What fun it would be if we could make the Lady
Principal pay 100*l.*! I'm sure it would only serve her right.

The beauty of it is, Nelly, she says she only looks at the
signatures of the letters that come here, to see if they are from
proper persons. This is very likely! How, then, *does she
know all that is going on in the girl's homes, if she never reads
their letters?* I've no patience with her! I'm sure I shall
never be able to look the mean creature in the face again.

Now, Nelly, I must tell you all about the young ladies; for I may not have another opportunity, dearest, of smuggling out a letter.

Well, then, when we went to breakfast, Mrs. Rodwell was seated on a sort of raised throne at the end of the table, and all the girl's walked up to her to curtsey, and "*Souhaiter le bon jour, Madama,*" and show her—this is a positive fact, dearest—their teeth and nails! Meggy told me, this was to teach us to keep them sharp and in good fighting condition, as *woman's natural weapons;* but she was only laughing at me, for I learnt afterwards it was to see that they were properly cleaned every morning. But I think the practice might well be dispensed with, as not being over and above complimentary to young ladies!

When my turn came, I was preparing to show my teeth in real earnest—for I felt both indignant and ashamed of such treatment—when she took me kindly by the hand, and instantly, at that touch of kindness, my mouth shut of its own accord. She asked me how I had slept, and introduced me to Miss Plodder, who, she said, would cheer my spirits and make me feel more at home. She is such a fat, round, little sleepy, and looks as stupid, too, as she is fat! If my spirits have to wait for Miss Plodder to cheer them, I'm afraid they'll have to wait long enough.

Well, my own darling Nell knows I am not dainty, and that I should think it wicked to be fanciful over good food; but I never did see such thick slices of bread, smeared over with what they called butter. I have not been so petted at home as to quarrel at any time with my bread and butter; but, on my word, I should as soon have thought of munching a deal board, as taking up one of the long slices—planks, rather—that were piled up, as in a timber yard, before me; and yet, to see the poor hungry girls! If it had been wedding-cake, they could not have devoured it more greedily!

I thought of the dear delicious hot rolls, soaked through and through with the best Fresh (at elevenpence a pound) that I had

been in the habit of having every morning for breakfast, and
sighed that I was not at home.

Meggy asked me which I liked best, "*hay or beans?*" Before I could answer that I had never tasted either, the Lady
Principal inquired "if I took cocoa or coffee?" A basin of the
latter was brought to me, but unless I had been told it was
coffee, I'm sure I should never have guessed it. It looked more
like water taken from the Regent's-canal. Meggy whispered
into my ear, "Hay's best;" and seeing me puzzled, she explained, shortly afterwards, that in their school dictionary hay
meant cocoa, and that beans was the English for coffee, from a
popular belief, which she said, "was extremely well grounded"
(in their coffee cups), that those agricultural commodities
formed the principal ingredients of their matutinal beverages.

Meggy Sharpe is such a nice girl, so clever and so full of
fun, and such large bright black eyes, and a face laughing all
over with mischief; it puts one in good humour merely to look
at it. I feel I shall love her very much, but not so much as
you, dearest Nelly.

After breakfast she told Miss Plodder that she would "take
care of me, and introduce me to the Elders." Then bidding
me not to be afraid, she led me by the hand to a group of tall
young ladies, and in a set speech, delivered in a mock tone,
such as I've heard my brothers imitate Mr. Charles Kean in,
" begged to present a humble candidate to their friendship and
favour." The tallest, a Miss Noble, who seemed the head
girl, and as stiff as a backboard, made me welcome, and then
began questioning me in the following manner :—" Did I live
in London?—at the West-end, of course?—perhaps in Bel-
grave-square? No! then near Hyde Park? No! then in
one of the Squares? Yes! Well, some of the Squares were
still respectable. In which of the Squares did I live, pray?"

I mumbled out, as well as I could, "Torrington-square."

" Oh! hem! where was Torrington-square?" continued my
tormentor. " Near the City, was it not? No!—what, near

Russell-square and Gower-street? Gower-street! Well, really, she knew nothing of those parts of the town."

I was next asked, "Whether my mamma went to Court." "No," I answered, in my ignorance; "but Papa does sometimes, and takes his blue bag with him when he has law business." This gave rise to shouts of laughter, and long exclamations of "Dear, dear!" whilst looks of pity were showered down upon me.

"I mean," continued Miss Noble, "her Majesty's receptions. My mamma goes to Court; and I am to be presented myself by the Grand Duchess of Mechlenburgh-Sedlitz immediately on my leaving College;" and she tossed her head up to the ceiling, until I thought it would never come down again.

"How did you come last night?" resumed Miss Noble. "In the omnibus," cried out wicked Meggy, who immediately ran away. "No; I know how she came," said another beauty, "for I was in the drawing-room at the time, and looked out of the window; she came in a clarence *with one horse*." And they all tittered again, and I felt my cheeks growing red, though why I should be ashamed of mamma's pretty clarence I don't know, even though it has but *one* horse.

I was next asked, "Whether my paternal (meaning papa, I suppose) lived at home?" "Of course," I answered; "where should he live?" "Why some people have an establishment in the city, and a family in a square. The shop (and they tittered again) must not be neglected." "Do not be rude, Miss Ogle," interrupted Miss Noble, affecting to be very serious; "personalities are extremely rude; and, besides, Miss Clover's father may not live in a shop. Tell us, dear, what profession are you in?" "I—I'm in no profession," I said, trembling lest I should be laughed at again. "Dear! what beautiful simplicity!" said the Court lady, lifting her hands up; "not you—your father, child." "Oh! papa is a stockbroker." "A what? A stockbroker! Pray what's that?" "I know," said the young lady who had told about the

clarence with one horse; "it's a trade; for I hear papa
talk of desiring his stockbroker to buy and sell; and I am
certain, now I think of it, that they deal in *bears and ducks.*"
"No such thing," exclaimed a little girl with a turn-up nose,
"they sell old stocks, such as bankrupts' stocks, or retiring
haberdashers' stocks; they're a sort of old-clothesmen." "At
any rate, they are not professional, and therefore must be in
trade," decided proud Miss Noble; and they all turned away
from me, with sneers and contempt. "It's no such thing," I
burst out; "my papa is a gentleman—a real gentleman—and
he's quite as good, if not better, than any of your papas, though
you are so proud: and I shan't answer any more of your rude
questions." "That's right," laughed Meggy; "that's the
way to disappoint them. Don't tell 'em anything."

You should have heard, too, Nelly, their curiosity about my
brothers, making me describe them over and over again—their
eyes, whiskers, noses, and calling them by their names, Oscar,
Alfred, Augustus, Walter, as if they had known them for
years. The impudent girl, with the turn-up nose, actually said
she felt she could madly love Oscar; and I couldn't help
replying, "You need not trouble yourself, Miss; he'll never
ask you." Silly thing! I'm sure Oscar wouldn't as much as
look at her—not even in church.

But the greatest shame has yet to come. You can never
believe what I am going to tell you, Nelly, although you know
I scorn fibbing!

Class had just broken up, when a maid came in carrying a
large tray; and only imagine my confusion when I saw laid
out on it all my cakes and goodies! Miss Blight (the quiet
teacher who had brought me into the schoolroom) called me,
and I was going to ask for permission to put them into my
play-trunk, when—think of my surprise, Nelly!—if she did
not actually seize *my plum-cake, and begin cutting it up into
thin slices!* At first I was so shocked that I could not speak;
and I was about to stop her, when she cut some large slices,

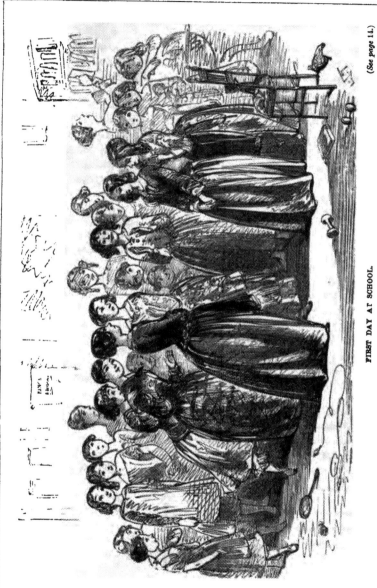

FIRST DAY AT SCHOOL.

(See page 14.)

and desired me "to hand them to the governesses, and then take the dish round to each young lady." I am afraid I looked vexed, and, in truth, I was nearly choking with passion; and I am sure you would have done the same, Nelly, for you would have seen no joke in treating girls to your goodies, after they had been making fun of you, and turning your papa and mamma into ridicule. But this was not all; for one rude thing, upon ascertaining from me that mamma made it, said, in a voice running over with vinegar, "I thought so, for she has forgotten the plums." Then my oranges were cut into quarters, and I had to hand them round also (*the governesses had halves!*) until all was gone, and I had only two pieces myself as a favour. Now, don't think me greedy, Nelly—you know I don't care for feasting, only I do not like to be forced to be generous, and to give to all alike, whether I like them or not—offering as much to that proud Miss Noble (who is not too proud, however, to eat another girl's cake) as to dear Meggy. I dare say it is very pleasant when it's not your own—"share and share alike" is all very fine; but I should like to know when their goodies are coming? As I am the last girl entering this term, I suppose it won't be before next half-year? And I mean to say, Nelly, it is most heart-rending—putting insult on the top of cruelty — to force you to help the governesses and *to double shares,* too, whilst I'm sure my slice broke all to pieces, it was so miserably thin.

Oh, dear, there's Mrs. Rodwell. If she catches me writing, I shall be found out; so my own darling Nelly, I must say good bye. Mind you write soon, and tell me all about dear S. Has he asked after me? and often? Is he pale? Tell him not to forget your devoted, true-hearted

KITTY CLOVER.

P.S.—Oh! Nelly, I have had such a fright; my heart is jumping up and down like a canary in a cage when the cat's underneath it. Only think of the Lady Principal's coming up

to my desk. I made sure it was to ask me for this letter, and
I determined in my mind to swallow it sooner than let her read
it. But, thank goodness! it was only to say she had not
opened my last letter to you, as it was sealed ; but, for the
future, she would close them herself, after looking over their
contents. Much obliged! Catch me giving her any other
than my own compositions. So darling we are safe ; but
isn't it lucky ?

P.S.—I'm sure you'll never be able to read this scrawl.
Why didn't you answer my last ?

THE THIRD LETTER LEFT.

(*No date, and post-mark illegible.*)

SHOWING HOW KITTY WAS MARRIED, AND THE CONSEQUENCES
OF THAT IMPRUDENT STEP.

DEAR mamma came yesterday, looking so happy and beautiful. I really believe she loves me, Nelly, for she smothered
me in kisses, until I thought I should never get my breath
again. I wanted to cry, and give her a good cuddle, and tell
her how much I loved her, and how I hated the college, and
everything in it ; but there sat Mrs. Rodwell the whole time,
in a new cap and black gloves, just as if mamma had come to
see *her*, and not me. And only to hear her high-flown speeches
about "my backwardness" and her "infallible system for
the development of every neglected faculty," and I don't know
what else! It gives me the fidgets merely to think of it.

Martha (kiss my dear sister for me) brought me your sweet
letter, my darling Eleanor, and I have worn it in my bosom ever
since, and I am determined, Nelly, to keep it there as long as I
live ; but, unfortunately, from reading it so often, or from some
cause or other, it has broken at all the edges, and I have been

obliged to stitch the several pieces together, so much so that I am sadly afraid it will scarcely last another week.

I knew your kind loving heart would feel for the wretchedness of your own suffering Kitty ; but you will rejoice to hear, darling, that, now I know some of the girls, I am a little more cheerful, and at times almost catch myself laughing. School s not such a wretched place *when you get used to it.* But I'll tell you all about it.

What do you think, Nell ? They have such a strange fashion here. They do not ask you to be friends, *but they marry !* Two young girls who are fond of each other *become husband and wife.* I could not tell what Meggy Sharpe meant when she "popped the question," and asked me to be "her little wifey." Then she laughed at my astonishment ; but that's nothing new for Meg, for she's always laughing ; and, when I asked her what she meant, she called me " her dear Sillyninny ;" so I determined to find out the secret myself. Well, my pretty Nell will never guess the meaning of all this, and so I suppose I must tell her.

The first thing after we had exchanged presents (I gave Maggy my gold locket and she gave me a silver thimble—*it was terribly bent, though*) she asked me for my purse, saying, that " husbands always kept the money, but I could have some when I wanted it. This was always the case in matrimony, all the world over." Then, of course, I must tell her all my secrets, as there was no real happiness in marriage unless there was perfect confidence between husband and wife, and she would afterwards tell me lots of things. So I told her of your being my bosom friend, Nelly ; but she said "that was nothing," and, I don't know how, but from question to question she got all out of me concerning dear S. (I mean Sydney) ; and—and —can you believe it ? Meggy has not only got a sweetheart, but is actually engaged to her cousin, a handsome young midshipman, at present braving the dangers of the wild ocean. She has got a lock of his hair (it's black) tied up with blue

c

ribbon in a true sailor's knot; and they are to be married as
soon as he is an admiral and rich enough.   Isn't she a lucky
girl, Nelly?

But I didn't like Meggy's quizzing me merely because I
blushed when I mentioned the dear name of Sydney.   I thought
it was very unfeeling, to say the least of it; though she did
say I should soon lose that stupid habit before I had been at
school a month.   She used to blush herself once, she told me,
but that was previous to her receiving so many offers!   And,
oh! Nelly, she showed me such a beautiful love-letter (I trembled like the deck of a steamer as she read it to me).   It was
from a sweetheart who almost died for her, only he was forced
to marry some one else for money.   He was a poet, in a
Government office, and his signature was written with his own
blood—only I must say it *looked uncommonly like red ink*.   But
Meggy knows he is miserable for life; for the last time she
met him he was dressed from his hat to his boots in black,
with the exception of his trousers, which were of a light spinach
colour.   Poor fellow! he's greatly to be pitied; and it's a
wonder to me how Meg can be so unconcerned about him.

I can't think how it could interest Meggy—but she was so
curious about Mamma and Papa, and my brothers, making me
tell her all I could remember about home and the servants, and
what we had for dinner, and whom we visited, and who visited
us.   Then I showed her my desk and work-box; and she took
them under her care, with my hair oils and scent-bottles (full
of scent), and pretty neck-ribbons, and gloves, and mittens,
and said she would look after them, for *fear I should lose them;*
declaring that, as she was my husband, she must protect me,
and fight all my battles; whilst on the other side, I am to help
her as much as I can by waiting on her, mending her linen,
spreading out her curl-papers, and keeping her drawers tidy.
I do not like to refuse, but I think I could have kept my own
stores just as well as she can.   We are to share everything.
As her wife, she said, everything that was mine was hers; and

she is carrying out this law, I must say, with the strictest impartiality, for I have scarcely a thing left.   On the other hand, she assures me that all she has is mine, though I do not see how I am to benefit much by this acquisition of property ; for I have looked into her drawers, and found nothing worth taking, except an old silk stocking.   If this is a foretaste of matrimony, Nelly, I hope I shall always remain single ; but—but, for goodness' sake, do not tell dear Sydney so.   It would only make him unhappy.

There is one consolation, my gloves (the best Jouvins) cannot be of much assistance to my unscrupulous lord and master, Miss Margaret Sharpe ; for, whilst my hand is, as you know 6¼, *his* must be at least 7½.

Another peculiarity of this "College life" is calling each other by your surname.   Your loving Kitty is never called Kitty, but always Clover ; and Meggy is always saluted Sharpe—without the Miss.   You cannot think how boyish and rude it sounds !

Now, Nelly, if my husband will excuse my running away from her, I intend to give you what I call a cat's-eye view of the principal girls.

Noble (the dignified one) is the queen of the school, and head monitress.   They all look up to her with awe, for she knows one of the maids of honour, and has an aunt who goes to Almack's.   Her guardian (Meggy tells me that it is her father ; but he's called her guardian, which is more than I can understand), Lord Lovime, drives to the College in a beautiful mail phaeton, with a dear little tiger, so tiny, you might put him in your muff, Nelly.   She is considered very elegant, and walks about the playground with her gloves and parasol.   She calls eating vulgar, but I'm sure she eats as much as any one.   She says it takes four generations to make a lady, is exceedingly bitter against all trades and shops, and declares that half the girls at college *haven't a drop of blood in their veins* ; and yet, to look at Miss Smiffel, the butcher's daughter, Nell, you

c 2

would imagine she was full of nothing else—she is as red in
the face as the lamp over a surgeon's door.

I don't know, but I don't like Miss Noble, with all her gran-
deur, and her gold fork and spoon with the magnificent crest
upon them. She is disdainful, and without pity to any one who
doesn't keep a carriage, and as servile to those who do—but
then it *must have two horses.* Her features are certainly handsome, but as cold as marble. To look at her, you would
imagine it was the head of some beautiful bust; and it's a
great pity she ever speaks, for it spoils the illusion. I almost
pity her, though, Nelly, for she seems so lonely on the pedestal
upon which she has taken her stand, and from which she never
descends. Her dignity draws around her a circle (an aristo-
cratic circle, I suppose she would call it), into which no one
ever thinks of stepping. All I know is, I would not exchange
my own dear fond Papa and Mamma for the whole bunch of her
fine relations, whose proud titles are all she cares for. She
calls home, and kissing, and love, and affection, all " vulgar
weaknesses," very well for the lower classes; and it is lucky
she thinks so, for I doubt if she has ever felt their sweet influ-
ence, or knows what it is to love devotedly as I do my sweet
Nelly, or S.

Noble's wife (you see I have already fallen into the College
habit of calling girls by their surnames) is Rosa Peacock.
Rosa is the beauty, the *belle,* of the school; and, as far as
beauty goes, she certainly deserves the title. She is the
daughter of Sir Hercules Peacock, who was a captain in the
body of Gentlemen-at-Arms (what kind of gentlemen are they,
Nell?) in the time of George IV., and quite an Adonis in his
day, and also (so Meggy says) a cheesemonger. Peacock is
certainly a lovely creature, tall and majestic, such as we have
only seen in the crush-room, Nelly, when we have been coming
out of the opera. Her hair is light, and falls in close curls,
which droop into the shape of wings on each side of her face,
as if it were too pretty for this world, and they wanted to carry

POMP AND VANITY.

(See page 21.)

it up to heaven. Then she has large die-away eyes, of the colour (excuse me, pet) of what we used, when little girls, to call sky-blue ; but then they are a very rich sky-blue, like *those pretty muslins which won't be washed.* But pretty as Peacock is—and I can tell you the school is rather proud of her—it is a thousand pities she is so conscious of her own beauty. She seems to be always saying, " Pray admire me." It is lucky she doesn't sleep in our bedroom, with only the one looking-glass, or else none of us would ever be able to get a peep at it. She is as full of her own charms as Noble is of her dignity. Meggy calls them *Pomp and Vanity,* and says it is all outside show, like the shops in the Lowther Arcade. They ought to be in the second class, or perhaps the third, only the Lady Principal favours them. She puffs them off, and hands them about as " show girls ;" and they would be sure to be disliked for that circumstance alone, if for no other. But the truth is they are so disagreeable, their pride is so offensive, that I doubt if they can point to a single friend in the whole school. The consequence is, they are driven to each other's society, and you will see them of a half holiday walking round our little bit of a playground arm-in-arm, turning their noses up at every one, and studying " Debrett's Peerage" together.

But, Nelly, I must leave you. My *husband* is calling me to mend her stockings, and I daren't disobey. What a little stupid I was ever to get married ! In frantic haste, your loving, miserable

KITTY CLOVER.

P.S. Excuse this wretched scrawl.

P.S. You tell me nothing about dear S.

P.S. The housemaid has consented to drop this in the post for sixpence.

THE FOURTH LETTER LEFT.

(Dated March 3rd.)

SHOWING WHAT KITTY THOUGHT OF SOME OF HER
SCHOOLFELLOWS.

I DO begin, Nelly, to like this wretched place a little better.
All the girls are not Nobles and Peacocks ; and it's lucky
they ain't, for I never met with such a couple of disagreeable
things. They set themselves up for great judges and wits,
ridiculing everything they do not like, and trying to make the
rest feel humbled and worthless, because our Mas have never
been to court, or our Pas do not drive a pair of horses !

Meggy Sharpe and I both think Annie Flower much prettier
than Rosa Peacock, although she is not a fine lady, and her
father is only a farmer. They call her "Dairymaid ;" but, for
all that, Miss Rosa Peacock is jealous of her beautiful complexion; and is always imitating Annie's merry laugh.

That little impudent thing with the turn-up nose is a Miss
St. Ledger. Her Pa is a City Alderman, and a great patron of
Mrs. Rodwell. Meggy calls her "Piggy,'' because she is always
stuffing—hiding in the closets and the box-room to eat *by
herself*, the things she smuggles into the College. Whenever
you meet her in the passages, she cannot speak—her cheeks
are crammed so full of goodies. They tell a story against her
about the drawing-room piano. It was terribly out of tune,
and upon examination was found to be full of orange-peel and
peach-stones. The supposition is that Miss St. Ledger had
taken the peaches and oranges up with her to be able to eat
them *on the sly* when she was practising, and, being suddenly
disturbed, had thrown them inside the lid of the grand piano,

so as not to be detected. This greedy girl is extremely rich, and she is always boasting that her Papa could buy up a whole street of such poor creatures as Noble and Peacock, who, she says, have *nothing but debts for a fortune, and a title to pay them off with.* At the same time she flatters them, and tries all she can to get friendly with them, but they only *snub* her the more. But Nelly, she dresses so beautifully, always in silks, and her pocket-handkerchiefs are as fine as muslin, and, I'm speaking the truth, trimmed with real *Valenciennes!* It makes you quite curious to finger them. Then she has boxes upon boxes full of the most lovely ribbons and belts ; whilst Madame La Vautrien makes her bonnets, and charges three guineas apiece for them! But in spite of all her finery, she is the meanest girl in the school—so stingy and greedy, always borrowing, and never lending—never sharing, never helping any one. I do not like her a bit—nasty, disagreeable thing! if she did not go and pry into my boxes ; and I heard her telling the girls "all was cheap and common—only one silk dress, and that a turned one of mamma's." The Lady Principal is very fond of her (her money, more likely), and is always sending her into the drawing-room to practise (though she can't play a bit), because she is so fat and fine, and has hot-house grapes sent to her.

Miss Plodder is another favourite. She is the "Good Girl." Her nickname is "Preterpluperfect." Poor girl, her face makes you sad to look at it. It seems full of tasks and forfeits. Her fingers are always inky ; and her hand is so cold, that touching it is as unpleasant as the tearing of silk. My blood runs cold merely to think of it. She never plays or laughs, but is always thumbing her lessons, though what she does with her learning no one can tell, for she is never "up" in class, and is always sent "down" at examinations.

How different is dear Lucy Wilde! She seems to know everything without looking at a book. It comes as naturally to her as eating. Ah! she is clever. The professors pay her such compliments before all the school, and the governesses are afraid of her. The Lady Principal, however, cannot bear Lucy, because she is idle, and up to fun. She tries to keep her down ; but Lucy is like a cork in a pail, she is sure to come to the top again. The more she is pushed under, the more she rises. With all her mad-cap tricks, she is always at the head of the class. How she learns no one can tell, for she is never seen with a book. Meggy says it comes to her in her sleep. Professor Drudge told us last week that if Lucy could only be tamed into studying she could do anything, and I believe it. She writes verses, too—little satirical poems on the mistresses, and Peacock and Noble ; and sent off on Tuesday the most beautiful Valentine I think I ever read.

But, Nelly, it is Amy Darling you would love best—a bright, pleasant girl, all sunshine, except when she cries, and she cries immediately any one is hurt. We all run to Amy directly we are in trouble. She is like a young mother to us, and treats us with such tenderness, that it is almost a pleasure to be in trouble to be comforted by Amy. She consoles one *so* beautifully, and I'm sure if our puddings were taken away we should miss them far less than the absence of dearest Amy. You should see how the little girls crowd round her in the playhouse, and pull her about. She romps with them with the greatest good-humour, and never tires in teaching the little things some new game. She was in bed for three days once, and any one would have imagined there was a death in the house ; but when she recovered, we made so much noise that the Lady Principal came down from her boudoir to inquire what was the matter. It's strange ! She is not clever, nor altogether pretty nor even professional (her papa's a coachmaker), and yet, somehow, notwithstanding these tremendous drawbacks, she is the favourite of all the school. Even the masters and schoolmistresses cannot help giving the preference to Amy. Professor Drudge himself, who seems to love nothing in the world but his snuff-box, pats her occasionally on the head, bestowing on her at the same time *a grim snuffy smile*, that he accords to no one else.

THE PEACEMAKER, THAT ALL ABIDE BY.

(See page 25.)

She is such a dear, dear love ! so sweet—so full of joy and sympathy—that I really believe, Nelly, she was intended for an angel, and was only made a school-girl by mistake.   Her sweetness is best shown by the fact that Peacock and Noble never give themselves airs to her, though her father is but a coachmaker.   She would shame them out of their vulgarity without retorting a harsh word, and make them blush (if that was possible) by merely reproaching them kindly.   It is a wonder for a school, where there are so many girls, that not one of them is jealous of Amy.   Such a thing would appear unnatural. It would be like being jealous of your mother, or of a nurse who had tended you through a long illness.   We are too grateful to be jealous : for there is not a girl in the school, big or little, but who has some cause to be grateful to her.   The little girls she protects, and saves them from being bullied ; and the big ones she advises when they are in a mess, besides helping them through their tasks.   She is the protectress that all fly to—the peacemaker that all abide by (*even those in the wrong*) ; and the general *confidante* of us all, the poor misstresses included.   Meggy calls her our " Sister Confessor ;" and really it is terrible to think of the heap of secrets that must be piled up, as high as the boxes on a Margate steamer, upon her honour.   When you think, Nelly, it is as much as we can do to keep *one* secret, I wonder how Amy can breathe with such a load upon her breast !   Yet she carries it all as lightly as a fairy does her wand.

I cannot for the life of me imagine, Nelly, why she has chosen poor Mary Owen for her wife !   There never were two persons so widely different, and yet firmer friends.   Meggy says, " poor Mary Owen is in pawn to Mrs. Rodwell," which means that she has been left as security for a debt, as hopeless as any National one.

Years ago (so Meggy tells me) Mary's father—a captain in the army— left her at school, with directions that she was to learn everything, and no expense spared in her education.

With the exception of one or two small remittances, nothing has been heard of her father since. Year after year Mary grows paler and more sad, with not a friend in the world to cling to, but dearest Amy, who treats her more like a sister than anything else, being always by her side, as something told her that if the poor girl hadn't a crutch of some sort to lean upon, she would assuredly fall to the ground. The Lady Principal has lost all hope of Mary being ever claimed, or (worse still) of her bill being ever paid. This makes Mary's position all the more melancholy, for she is pointed to as a kind of living monument to the cardinal virtues of the schoolmistress who keeps her. If there is a little sermon on charity or benevolence, Mary is always chosen as its text. Whenever there is a lecture read about ingratitude, poor Mary is always brought forward as the disgraceful illustration of it. It is the same with dishonesty, *taradiddles*, fibbing, and the entire category of school vices—Mary serves as the example of them all. It would seem as if the poor girl was kept as a "terrible warning" to the College; and I'm sure in this capacity alone, that her bill has been paid more than twenty times over. It is sad to watch the poor girl while she's being thus publicly pointed at before her schoolfellows. She never says a word, nor attempts to defend herself. She sits quietly in her seat, her face growing paler, and her head falling lower with each blow of her accuser; and if you saw her heavy, tearless eye, Nelly, and her lips quite colourless, as I have seen them, you would pity her with all your heart, and long to go up and kiss her, and tell her not to mind it. Often and often have I felt inclined to call out and beg of Mrs. Rodwell to stop such cruelty; but fear has pinched my lips, and I have caught myself crying, and I defy any one to help it. But I don't mean to say that Mrs. Rodwell ill-treats Mary, or is positively unkind, or lifts her hand against her; but she is always taunting her with her misfortune in so sharp a manner, that I would sooner by far be beat outright, or be sent away at once. It is one

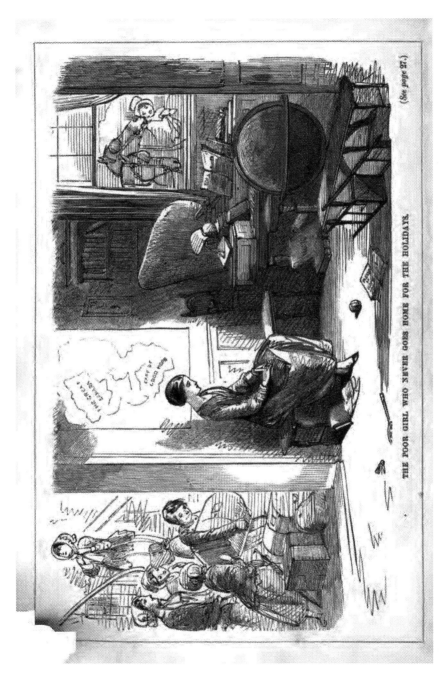

THE POOR BOY WHO GOES FROM HOME FOR THE HOLIDAY.

(See page 27.)

unceasing tyranny of little petty trifles all day long (a tyranny of pins and needles, Meggy calls it), which I call most cowardly for a woman like Mrs. Rodwell (though she has lost her money) to use against a poor girl who cannot defend herself; just as if Mary wouldn't pay if she could! On such occasions Amy is kinder to her than ever, and struggles, by dint of affection, and by trying to lead her into play, to make her forget the harshness she has experienced during school hours. I'm not certain that she succeeds very well. Mary tries, in grateful return for so much kindness, to smile and to play; but it isn't smiling nor playing, Nelly, it's working, and *hard working* at it.

Her dress is the funniest thing you ever saw. When I say funny, I do not mean it makes you laugh—far from it—but that it is extremely odd and peculiar. At first Mary used to wear the cast-off things of two Indian girls, who are here and never go home; but since she has grown tall she is packed up in Mrs. R's old trumpery finery, and flits about like a thin shadow of what the Lady Principal was six months previously. No one, however, is cruel enough to quiz Mary. Her sorrow throws a sacred protection over her that is better than any shield, and even Miss St. Ledger (with her pert turn-up nose) forgets the sharpness of her tongue in her presence. Amy, besides, wouldn't allow any one to slight her. They tell me, Nelly, that when " breaking-up day " comes round, and all are skipping about in the wild joy of being fetched home, poor Mary sits silently apart, shunning everybody—avoiding the windows where all the girls are heaped together, watching the arrival of the carriages; and that she almost runs away from dear Amy's caresses, rejecting her loving endeavours to cheer her, as if they were a source of pain to her. Dear Amy always stops the last with her; but, when it comes to her turn to go away, then poor Mary flings herself round her devoted friend's neck, and bursts into one long flood of tears, as if her heart was breaking. May we never know such grief as that, Nelly! Only think, dearest, how cheerless must the holidays be to the

poor homeless girl!   The re-assembling of school, which
school-girls dread so much, must come back to her with all the
delight of holidays to us.

Once Amy asked for Mary to go home with her, but the
Lady Principal objected to it.   It would take too much money
and trouble to "get her up."   Amy said she should wear her
things ; but Mrs. Rodwell still objected.   She was afraid
(Meggy says) to "trust the security of her debt out of
sight!"   Poor Mary has never left the Princesses' College
now for four years, except at such times when she has been
out walking with the school !

This is very sad and terrible, Nelly, and we ought to think
ourselves very fortunate that we have such good papas and
mammas, and that our positions in life are very different from
that of poor Mary Owen !   But I have written myself quite
miserable, and you too, I am afraid, Nelly, so no more at
present, dear, from

Your little stupid

KITTY CLOVER.

P.S. Excuse haste.
P.S. Why don't you write ?

THE FIFTH LETTER LEFT.

(*Dated March 9th.*)

SHOWING WHAT KITTY THOUGHT OF SOME MORE OF HER
SCHOOLFELLOWS.

IN my last letter I forgot to tell you about the two Miss Suetts,
Emilia and Julia.   They are fat, and round, and heavy,
like (Meggy says) a couple of yeast dumplings.   Their parents
are in India, and they never go home.   No one cares much
about that, however ; for they are great *teazes*, and the most

dreadful *tell-tales*. But they are never without preserves and pickles of some kind, and have such delicious pomegranates and guava jelly sent to them, in such large blue jars, that, after all, I doubt if any two girls would be more missed from the school than the two Suetts—disagreeable things as they are. You should only taste their tamarinds, Nell!

There is also Ada Steele, the poetess, who writes verses, some of which have actually appeared in print (in the *Family Page*, I think), and you cannot imagine how conceited she is about it. I am told she knows every line of poetry that ever was written. She is such a dreadful plague, that I never go near her if I can avoid it. You cannot ask her what's the day of the month, but she'll give you a hundred lines of poetry right off from some poet or other. Meggy calls her " a tap of poetry," which once turned on, will go on running till you stop it. Byron is her especial favourite, and she always calls him " dear." His works are not allowed in the College ; but Ada Steele has got a copy of them, and she puts it under her pillow every night.

˙ But the girl I dislike most is Susan Carney. Fancy a tall, thin creature, with hair the colour of blotting-paper, and with eyes like an owl's, that cannot look at you, and you have her standing before you. She is the " *sneak*" of the school ; and moves about like a cat. When we are talking secrets, and turn round, there she is—pretending to look for something, but in reality listening. Or, if a girl has comfortably got one of James's delicious novels inside her grammar, and looks up to see that it is all right and snug, there is Carney's cold fishy eye sure to be fixed sideways upon her. Meggy says her eye is so sharp, she's confident that, like a needle's, *it would cut thread*. We cannot have a bit of fun, but Miss Carney is sure to spoil it. We cannot read or write a letter in class without her knowing it. We cannot talk to the masters, or have a comfortable bit of gossip about the filthy dinners and the Lady Principal, without our being requested, before the day is half

over, "to step to Mrs. R.'s boudoir," after which you will see
the girls coming back with red eyes and burning cheeks.

The oddest thing is, no one is sure that it is Carney who tells,
though every one is convinced that she does. She manages it
so cleverly that she is never found out. We tease her as much
as we dare, calling her "policeman," "spy," "tell-tit," and
every thing we can think of; but it takes no effect upon her.
She turns a little pale, talks morality in a whining tone, and
leaves it to Mrs. Rodwell to redress her wrongs.

Another curious thing is the way in which she wheedles a
secret out of you. Though on your guard, she flatters and
fawns, and coaxes and lectures till you have parted with your
secret long before you are aware of it. You would imagine
she was chloroform, so cleverly does she extract it, without the
smallest consciousness on your part. The fact is, she *crawls
over you*, Nelly; and as for talking, it is my firm belief she
would talk a letter out of a letter-box. She is exceedingly
neat and clean, with not a single hair out of bounds ; and,
somehow, her dresses do not rustle, nor her shoes creak, as
other persons' do. She is down upon you, like a shower at the
horticultural *fête*, before you have time to run for it. What
with her crawling, and her sleek appearance, and her gliding
so noiselessly about the room, she looks like a big lizard, or
some slippery serpent, that was advancing towards you ; and I
always feel inclined to scream, or to put up my parasol, when
she comes near me, to frighten her away.

Nor is she much a favourite with the remainder of the school.
The little girls bribe her with oranges and cakes, and lend her
small sums of money, to prevent her telling. But the big girls
know it's no use, and waste nothing upon her : they know well
enough she will take the bribe one minute, and go and *blab* the
next. The governesses even are afraid of her, and begin talking of the weather whenever she approaches.

But what shocks me the most, Nelly, is that she is righteous.
She moans and groans, and turns up the whites (or the yellows,

rather) of her eyes, and is *so* pious at church, and is always inveighing against "the shameful wickedness" of the school. Then she reads hymns, and is embroidering a *prie-dieu* for her godpapa, who is something in the Church, and exceedingly rich; and she writes such insufferably long sermons, twice the length of anybody else's; and after service she begs to see Mrs. Rodwell, *pour confier son cœur* as she calls it, but we all know what that means, for, as sure as plum-pudding on Sundays, some one is sure to be punished that same afternoon! I only wish we could find her out in anything. I really believe the entire school would rush up to the Lady Principal, and tell of her. But Miss Carney is far too cautious to be caught tripping! They tell me she even sleeps with her eyes open.

Let us turn from this hateful creature (I can't help hating her, Nelly) to some more agreeable subject. I will not tire you with descriptions of Miss Smiffel, the butcher's daughter, or Miss Embden, the baker's daughter, except to tell you that they have a sad time of it, and are called rare ugly names, because their papas happen to be butchers and bakers, just as if they could help it. I need not tell you, either, about Lizzy Spree, a little, merry, fidgetty, laughing thing, with black eyes, who is the romp—the "bad girl" of the school. She is always playing tricks, making apple-pie beds, or sewing up the tops of our stockings, or hiding the dancing-master's shoes, or tying the cat's tail to the parrot's leg, or filling Miss Blight's bed with bread-crumbs and cockchafers, or breaking a window, or tearing her dress every day. The consequence is, she is always in punishment; but she cares no more for it than a duck cares for an umbrella. She spends all her pocket-money on crackers and detonating balls and valentines, and is always going to be expelled; only Mrs. Rodwell relents, and gives her "one chance more." The maid fell down-stairs with the soup-tureen yesterday, from the fact of her strewing the kitchen steps with marbles and orange-peel. It was too bad. We had to go without soup in consequence.

But, Nelly, you would quite love little Jessie Joy ; she is the
wee'st little thing you ever. You might hang her to your
châtelaine. You would declare that she was not more than ten,
and yet she was sixteen last birthday. She has a rosy round
face, and little flaxen curls, exactly like a pretty doll, if you
could only keep her still for a moment to look at her. She
plays about the room like the sun on a looking-glass, and her
whole body seems to quiver with light. I defy you to catch
her, unless, perhaps, it was in the dark. We call her " pet "
and " tiny."

I don't know how it is, Jessie cannot be taught ; and yet
she is far from being an idiot, for the little thing understands ;
nor is she stupid, for she is quick enough to outwit us all.
Still, they have never been able to teach her anything. Her
eyes (I don't know what colour they are) fly away like butter-
flies directly you attempt to catch them, and settle on all places
but on her book. We think she can read, but no one is sure
of it. If told to learn, she pouts her lips like cherries, until
you feel inclined to bite them ; and her little head swings to
and fro, Nelly, like the bells on a fuchsia, when set a dancing
by the wind. The Lady Principal cannot scold her. The
utmost she can do is to call her to her in an angry tone, when
she takes up her little head in her two hands as if it were a
bowl of milk, and kisses her gently on the forehead. This is
all her punishment ; and the little culprit runs back into her
place as quick as a rabbit.

But if she can't read, or spell, or learn, you should only
hear her sing, Nell ! It is like a wild bird. She warbles every
air she hears. Music seems to gush from her like water from
a fountain. Once she was caught playing, and they say it
sounded like the rejoicing of good spirits ; but she cried when
they wanted her to do it again, and has never touched the in-
strument since. She dances more like a fairy than a human
being. And yet when Monsieur Viaulon (the French dancing-
master) attempted to teach her the polka, she ran away and

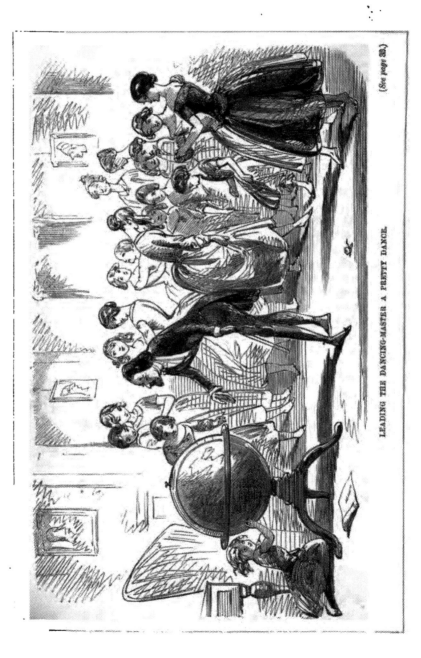

LEADING THE DANCING-MASTER A PRETTY DANCE.

(See page 53.)

hid herself behind the great globe in the music-room. The truth is, her dancing has nothing of the ball-room in it. She flits about so restlessly, it makes your eyes wink to look at her. Her feet never seem happy on the ground, and I always have a curious fear when the window is opened that Jessie will fly out of it.

The girls are rather frightened at her restless ways and her strange beauty, which seems to belong more to the air than to the earth. They declare that she is a fairy changeling ; and that the tale which is told of her father being shot in a duel, and of her mother dying when Jessie was born, is all a story. Jessie rarely goes home. The only person who comes to see her is an aged aunt, with a face all over lines, like a railway map. She brings her plenty of toys and plenty of sweeties ; but Jessie, apparently, does not care the least about her. The only person her flighty disposition stops in its giddy career to alight upon is Amy Darling. She listens to no one else without impatience—she will play with no one else, except it is a young kitten that belongs to the cook—she will obey no one. else. But then I believe if Amy spoke to the lightning, that she would stop it.

I am so tired of scribbling, dear Nelly, that I can't write any more to-day, though I could fill a whole band-box with particulars about this place. So no more at present from your dear affectionate

KITTY.

P.S. What do you think, Nelly! I've such bad news to tell you. That impudent Miss St. Ledger, with the turn-up nose, tells me that Margaret Sharpe (my husband) is nothing but deceit, and that she will turn me off as soon as she has got every thing she can out of me. I don't believe anything half so bad of my darling Meggy ; and I'm sure it's only a wicked nvention of that spiteful "Piggy."

P.S. But that is nothing to the following. Oh! Nelly,

D

Nelly dear, I'm afraid there'll soon be a speedy end to our correspondence ; Betsy, the housemaid, has just been telling me that she cannot put any more letters into the post under a shilling apiece. She says, if she was found out, it would be as much as her place was worth. Depend upon it, dearest, I will spend the last shilling I have in the world sooner than not write to you ; but what am I to do when all my money's gone ? To make matters worse, too, dear mamma gave me no money when she called last week. I suppose she forgot it. I wonder, if I was to ask the music-master (*he gave me a voice-lozenge yesterday*), whether he would drop them in the post for me ?

THE SIXTH LETTER LEFT.

(Written on Copy-book paper, and apparently left by hand.)

SHOWING WHAT KITTY THOUGHT OF GOVERNESSES IN GENERAL, AND ONE IN PARTICULAR.

NELLY, dearest, I have formed a great determination. Nothing shall ever induce me to become that poor, absurd, ill-used creature, called a governess. I would starve sooner, or make shirts (which is pretty nearly the same thing), or emigrate and marry the first savage I met, or be a " touter " at a bonnet shop, or even go into service at a cheap lodging-house ; anything, Nelly, sooner than be turned into that hopeless, spiritless, friendless being a governess seems destined by nature, or society, to be.

A governess in a private family is bad enough, but then she is not totally deprived of the comforts of home. She has a room, or at least a bed, entirely to herself, and her meals are generally the same as those of the family. Besides, a certain degree of respect is always paid to her. The servants are obliged to treat her with civility, *at all events in the presence of their mistresses ;* and the mistresses are compelled to show her a little attention, if it is only done to set a good example to their servants. Then, again, their " young charges " cannot invariably be amusing themselves at her expense. They cannot always be teasing her. When they are taken out for an airing in the carriage, or when they are brought down after dinner with their shiny faces and glossy ringlets, or whenever there is company, or their parents and strangers are present, the governess enjoys a brief respite from that system of petty tyrannies she is the untiring victim of elsewhere. She has her few pleasures, though perhaps they may come at long straggling intervals ; she has her distractions, her excitements in moving about in the world, and going to places of public amusements, and occasionally she knows what it is to enjoy the sweet success of rivalry—for have we not seen, Nelly, many a poor neglected governess who was doing the work of a musician at the piano, without his wages, receive in the course of the evening more attention than the fine young ladies themselves who were the worshipped idols of the establishment ?

But the governess in a girls' school has a very different life of it, Nelly. She hasn't a moment to herself. She is the first to rise, and the last to go to bed. She hasn't even the privacy of a bed-room to herself, for she is obliged to sleep in the same room as the girls, to look after them. The only privacy she knows is when she creeps into bed and draws the curtains round her. Our play-hours are no play-hours to her ; rather on the contrary, for then her torments really begin, and only end when the bell rings again for class. She is the target at which every little chit fires her fun, and thinks she has a perfect right to do so. She is the only game at which the girls never tire of playing, and to see how they enjoy it you would imagine there was no amusement like it. It is true, Nelly, I have not seen much misery yet, and hope I never shall ; but I can hardly imagine anything in this world *more miserable than a school governess on a half-holiday.*

Why, look at poor Blight. I have only to look upon her to feel for the sufferings of the whole class. Her nature seems to be sun-dried. She never smiles, and there is such an air of resignation about her, such a tone of despair that runs through all her words and smallest movements, that it is perfectly clear Hope never whispers into her ear any of those soft motherly words which soothe the agony of one's heart and lull it quietly off to sleep.

She may justly be called our " mistress of all work." She does a little of everything ; she helps the smallest girls to dress ; takes the junior pupils ; hears the reading ; sees to the wardrobes ; gives out the linen ; teaches needlework ; and superintends the Saturday night's cleaning ; in short, she is expected, as they say of servants, " to make herself generally useful," which means, in our instance, that she is worked to death by everybody, and spared by nobody ; besides being teased, deceived, bullied, and ridiculed by every one who has a fancy that way ; and for leading a life like this, she only gets 16l. a year and her board and lodging during the holidays !

Snapp (another of our teachers) smiles at Blight's old-fashioned learning. She says it is quite out of date, and only fit for a charity school. Mademoiselle (the French teacher) quizzes her dress, and makes fun of her melancholy, and talks of her contemptuously, as " ça," which I am told is the same as if you were speaking of a cook, or a poor relation, and called her " it." Fraulein (the German mistress) mimics her, and laughs over her patient endurance and old-maidish manners.

It must be confessed that poor Blight's appearance affords plenty of temptation for this cruel ridicule. She is certainly very ugly, and no one ever loses an opportunity of telling her so. The worst is, the example set by the schoolmistress is followed with the greatest zest by the school-girls, who indulge in all kinds of practical jokes at her expense. She is unfortunately very short-sighted, and consequently they are always hiding her spectacles, or else rubbing the glasses over with butter, or ink.   No one considers there is any harm in this, for the girls have grown to look upon Blight as " fair game ; " and if any one can put her into a passion, it is considered " rare fun," and thought just as harmless as throwing bread-pills at one another when the mistress's back is turned.   When there is no other amusement going on, the cry is always raised, " Let's go and tease Blight," and you see the whole school rushing forward as eagerly as if a gypsy suddenly appeared at the play-ground gate to tell us our fortunes.   But if any one is in trouble, Blight is the first to screen her.   If any girl is ill, Blight will sit up with her all night, and will pet and nurse the little sufferer until she almost fancies herself at home ; and when the little invalid has grown well again, and has recovered the use of her tongue and fingers, Blight never says a word about the ungrateful return, but bears it all like a martyr, which, in truth, she really is.   Ugly as she is, I really think there are times when I could *throw my arms round her neck, and kiss her for her goodness.*

I cannot tell you all the nicknames which they have for her face and person, nor would it altogether be agreeable for you, Nelly, I think to hear them.   Suffice it to say, the poor thing is very old—*thirty-nine*, if she is a day ; and she has the funniest little head of hair, every hair appearing to be pulled as tight, and to be almost as wide apart, as the strings of a harp. The top of her head is mounted with a round knot of hair no bigger than the worsted ball you see on a Scotch cap.   It's a wonder to me she doesn't wear a wig or a cap of some sort, though perhaps it would be too dangerous, as every one would undoubtedly be trying to pull it off.   The girls declare no one can recollect her having a new gown.   Every quarter a very thin, snuff-brown silk, on a very stiff lining, is brought out as Sunday best ; but it is only the old one turned and altered a bit, for that little wicked thing, Jessie Joy, put a drop of ink on one of the breadths on purpose to find it out ; and there it

is still, journeying about, backwards and forwards, first in front
and then behind ; now on the top, just under her chin, and
next down at the bottom, sweeping the floor, precisely as the
faded silk is twisted or turned to hide the creases and the.
ravages of old age.   The girls calculate the period they have
been at school by this venerable gown ; and it's no unusual
thing to hear them, when disputing about any particular date,
settling it at once by referring to the age of Miss Blight's
brown silk, saying, "I recollect very well it was in the ninth
quarter of Blight's Sunday gown ; " and a reference to a date
of this kind is considered as indisputable as to a Family Bible,
or an old almanack.

But these are small matters, Nelly, which I am half ashamed
to tell you, for under this poor garment there is a heart of so
much goodness as to make us wonder at the strange hiding-
places in which virtue sometimes delights in lurking, as if from
modesty it had taken every precaution not to be found out.
What do you think, Nelly ?   I am told by Meggy that poor
Blight supports an old bedridden mother !   She has no positive
proof of this, but she is morally sure of it.   This, then, accounts
for the reason why the poor governess is always working so
hard—never resting from crocheting purses, and knitting anti-
macassars sufficient to cover all the sofas in the world.   If
you ask her for whom she makes this extraordinary quantity
(you can't think, Nell, how quickly and beautifully she works),
she simply replies, her pale face becoming paler, "*for a dear
friend ;* " and that is all we can get out of her to reward our
vulgar curiosity.   This must be the truth, for at all hours,
both early and late, has she got a needle in her hand.   There
is a story that she wakes up sometimes in the middle of the
night, and works whilst the girls around her are sleeping.   But
no one knows the cause of her excessive industry, and I really
think she would only be miserable if it were known, and her
fingers would not ply their work of love half so nimbly if she
suspected that the girls, as they watched her with such fixed

curiosity, were acquainted with the sacred object for which she was toiling. It is a puzzle, when or where she sells all the things she finishes, and no one exactly likes to find out, though one or two attempts have been made, but always ending, I am happy to say, in the most complete failure. It makes me sad to watch her anxiety when there is a postman's knock at the door. She starts up in her seat, and pauses for a while in her work (the only pause it ever knows), until she gives out the letters ; and then you would pity her with all your heart to see how disappointed she is—what a vacancy of hope falls like a dark shadow upon her face—when she learns that there is not one for her ! Though when there is a letter it is scarcely any better. She sighs heavily, looks sometimes at a little locket she carries in her breast, and hurries on with her work quicker than ever, as if the purse she was finishing was to contain her own money instead of somebody else's, and she had so much that she wanted the use of it immediately.

If you have any fancy-work you want doing (any braces or cigar cases you wish to give away as presents), will you send it to me, Nelly, and I will ask Blight, if I can do so without offending her, to do it for me ?

I'm obliged to finish my letter, Nelly, for the fact is I have been writing the latter part of it in our bedroom with a piece of wax candle I took out of a candlestick there was in the hall, and there is only just sufficient left to enable me to scramble into bed, and to assure you how dearly you are loved by

Yours affectionately,

KITTY CLOVER.

P.S.—I intend that my bootlace shall come undone, some-where about the grocer's, when we are out a walking to-mor-row, so that I may lag behind, and drop this in the post unobserved. Oh ! dear—the candle's gone out. What sh——

THE SEVENTH LETTER LEFT.

(Dated April the 9th.)

SHOWING WHAT HAPPENED ON A VERY IMPORTANT DAY, AND
WHAT KITTY THOUGHT OF SOME OF HER MASTERS.

WELL, Nelly, it is all over with Sharpe and me. Our presents (or rather *my* presents) have been returned, our letters torn up, and the key of my box given back to me. You cannot imagine how spiteful the thing was. She reproached me with all the horrible crimes in the world, until at last I began to think I was the guiltiest creature under the sun, and actually got so frightened that I couldn't look at myself in the glass; but as the girls still played with me, and still borrowed my money, I thought I could not be so wicked after all. Accordingly, screwing up my courage, *as if I was about to take a pill,* I snapt my fingers at Miss Meggy, and have been a widow ever since. Catch me marrying again, that's all!

To-day, dearest Nelly, is the 14th of February. Not a girl, I believe, in the whole school, slept a wink last night; ever since sunrise, there has been such a humming and buzzing, exactly as you hear at church when the service is just over. I believe all the girls are mad. No one seems to care for fines or forfeits. What is twopence or sixpence, or a hundred lines of the " History of England," so long as a dear sweet valentine is smuggled into the College; and it requires all the art which a woman has of smuggling, to pass a letter through the examination of this place. I declare it's worse than the Custom-house, when you land from Boulogne. Every one who comes in has his pockets searched, and the Lady Principal stands on the staircase all day, watching for the postman. She little knows, however, that he has been bribed (*with half a dozen* SILVER THIMBLES) to slip all the letters under the door without that tell-tale " tat-tat ; " or that Susan has earned in one day more ribbons and handkerchiefs than a year's wages would buy her, simply by having a little human feeling. Snapp and the Lady Principal were never fluttered with such hopes, I'll be bound, when they were young, although it is so long ago, they may well be excused for forgetting it.

But it does not matter, Nelly, their locking us up in a state of siege. Rosy May has got a beauty sent round her bottle of strengthening mixture by the doctor's handsome young man ; and Lucy Wilde found such a duck tucked in her stockings from the wash. And those impudent fellows next door have pelted us over the garden wall with half a dozen all tied on to a piece of string precisely as if it were the tail of a kite that had got entangled in the trees.

And then, Nelly (mind this is a secret) there came a new Sunday dress for me (a beautiful shot silk, with all kinds of colours, just like mother-o'-pearl) ; and what do you think ? there, inside it, hid up the sleeve, was such a love of a valentine for your dear, happy, happy, Kitty ! Oh gracious ! when I opened it, I saw two sweet little doves, as white as bride-cake, caged in a net of beautiful silver paper, hovering over a large heart, smothered, dear, in the sweetest roses ! It was so pretty, you can't tell ; and I was *so* happy I could have gone to bed and have cried the rest of the afternoon. How kind of *him* to think of me on such a day ! Bless him ! how foolishly I love him to be sure, and I should be very wicked if I didn't ; for it was only yesterday I flung the paring of an apple three times round my head, and when it had fallen on the ground, there it was in the form of the dear letter " S ! " You understand, dearest, but not a word !

Snapp had one. It was inside an orange that was thrown at her from over the wall. Those impudent boys again ! She tore it up most indignantly, and flung the bits away with a burst.

of eloquence about "the vulgar ribaldry of such ignorant, witless insults." We picked up the bits afterwards, and, putting them together, found they formed the ugliest picture that ever was seen, of an old witch riding on a birch-broom, with a big bottle in her hand. It was too bad, but we have pasted the pieces on a sheet of paper, and intend to keep it by us to spite her with some day, if she is unkind to us.

The fact is the whole house is crazy. If it was breaking-up day there couldn't be more fun and less discipline. Even that long piece of dryness, Miss Twigg, has been caught laughing several times, and the servants have been giggling up and down stairs, and all over the house, and running every minute to the door, until at last Mrs. Rodwell has put the chain up, and says she'll answer the door herself. She's in such a passion that I shouldn't like to be one of those poor girls who havn't paid for their last half year, and to be taken up before her !

Even that curious old Mr. Penn has become touched with the infection. He has been setting us the drollest copies, about "Faint Heart ne'er won Fair Lady," and "Though Lost to Sight, to Memory Dear," and such like ; exceeding even his usual eccentricities.

He is the funniest little specimen you ever saw, Nelly, and ought to sit to have his portrait taken in China. He would make a capital Dresden ornament, for he is a very great curiosity ; but in his present shape he is much more curious than ornamental. He is our writing-master ; but his accomplishments go far beyond pot-hooks and hangers ; for he teaches us, also, arithmetic, mathematics (much we understand about them !), and Latin (we all like "Amo, I love "—I think of Sydney as I conjugate it), and elocution ; besides drawing to the juniors. Poor Penn ! His is a sad life, Nell. He was brought up with expectations of having a large fortune. Those expectations are all gone now ; for you cannot read the slightest hope in his care-worn face. His whole appearance implies a struggle to live. Every article of his dress speaks of a long fight with poverty. His coat looks so thin, that you imagine if it were brushed, it would be swept clean away like so much dust. It is buttoned close up to his throat ; and what you see of his linen is clean, though rough and jagged at the edges, like the leaves of a book that's been badly cut. His boots are patched to that extent that, when it has been raining very hard, he doesn't like drying them at the fire, for fear of our laughing at the numerous patches about them. His hat——but never mind about his dress, Nelly ; for I feel a sort of shame in counting the darns and stitches about this poor fellow's appearance. Suffice it to say, he always looks the gentleman in the midst of his shabbiness, and that he wins the respect of us giddy little girls, even in spite of his bad clothes. The latter, I can tell you, is no small recommendation in a girl's school.

He is clever, and I would sooner learn of him than of that ponderous Professor Drudge, whose explanations are so high-flown that we never can see what they mean, *even by standing on tiptoe*. At first, all manner of tricks were played upon old Penn. He never could find his spectacles—his knife was always mislaid—his quills were always stolen—but he never grumbled or made the slightest complaint. Last winter he used repeatedly to leave the room. We could not fancy why or where he went, until one day he dropt his pocket-handkerchief. It was nothing but holes and rags—almost as bad as the handkerchief I have seen the clown in a pantomime wipe his eyes with when he has pretended to be crying. He had been ashamed to withdraw it in our presence ; and well he might, for on my word, without meaning any harm, we should all have burst out laughing, if he had. We could not have helped it, Nelly. You never saw such a thing, dear ! "It was not a pocket-handkerchief," said that great stupid Meggy Sharpe, "so much as a Penn-wiper ! "

Well! as we were all laughing at its poverty and comical appearance—you must have laughed yourself, Nelly—who should come in but Blight ? In a few strong words she

made us ashamed of our unfeeling mirth, and brought the
colour still more to our tingling cheeks by running up stairs
and bringing down one of her own pocket-handkerchiefs, which
she bade us slip unperceived into poor old Penn's coat pocket.
We watched him from the window. The old gentleman pulled
out his handkerchief as soon as he left the house, but, per-
ceiving the substitution, his head dropt, poor fellow, and we
saw him with the handkerchief held up to his eyes until he
turned the corner.

Ever since then, no more tricks have been played with our
writing-master. His poverty, unlike with most men, has been
his friend—and a very good friend too. Contributions have
been dropt in the same poor-box for his relief, until the old
gentleman has grown comparatively quite a dandy ; one of
Noble's black satin aprons has found him in stocks for months,
and Blight is always knitting comfortable muffetees, slippers,
and chest-protectors for him in the winter. We picture to
ourselves the old man emptying his pockets when he gets home,
and his surprise at finding the little gifts (and cake sometimes)
they contain. We are happy in the pleasure we know we
give him. He never says a word, but merely looks his thanks.
We feel his gratitude in the increased kindness we receive from
him. He calls us "his angels," and we know directly what
he means ; if he said more, O Lord! how we should all cry,
and he, perhaps, more than any of us.

He is here, Nelly, mostly all day long ; but doesn't dine
with us. The Lady Principal sends him out a plateful, heaped
up with almost insulting profusion, as if she were sending it
out to a beggar. Perhaps she isn't wrong, however, for it is
all eaten. He carries down the tray himself, that none may
see how cleanly his plate has been cleared.

I need not tell you, Nell, dear, that we all are fond of poor
Penn. He is so kind, so gentlemanly, so patient, acting to us
more like a parent than a teacher. Besides, he sets us the
strangest copies, the oddest problems—things never heard of

in a school before—but reconciling us to our tasks by making us laugh, and interesting the dullest pupil.   You won't credit it, but that conceited thing Twigg fancies him in love with her. She dresses out her ringlets as long as spaniel's ears, and puts on cherry neck-ribbons when he comes.   All day long is she pestering him to mend her pen, and to explain away difficulties about x in algebra ; just as if a man could be bothered into love !   Penn takes it all very good-temperedly, but I imagine it would bring his wig prematurely to the grave, if he was told that he was going to marry Twigg.

None of us can tell what pittance the Princess' College gives for the life-service of such a man.   Not a tenth, I will be flogged, of what they give to Herr Hullabullützer.   Such fuss, dear, as is made for the Herr's reception.   The room is heated to a certain degree of nicety, the light is subdued, sherry and biscuits are ready for his refreshment, tea and cake (*our cake*) brought in afterwards, and the young ladies kept waiting in succession every quarter of an hour, so as not to lose a moment of his valuable time.   And you should only see him lounging in the arm chair ; his little fourpenny-piece of a watch placed before him, as if the object of his visit was to follow its hands, and not our fingers.   Why, he looks, dear, the handsomest personification of contentment, hair-oil, and conceit, that a foreigner ever *bamboozled* people with in this country.   His shirt is light pink, and perforated like an openwork jam-tart.   His wristbands are turned back nearly as much as the sheet on the pillow of a bed.   His head would make a beautiful block for a French hair-dresser's window ; and he has sufficient chains and miniature pistols, donkeys, cannons, and dogs dangling round his neck to start in business a Jew pedlar.   He dozes one half the time ; but then it is a reverie—the meditation of genius. The other half he plays with his glossy curls or his whitey-brown moustache, and so he may well be excused if he doesn't know exactly to a minute what air his pupil is playing.   It's true, he scarely gives himself the trouble to correct us when we are wrong ; but then he teaches the young Princesses ! and so we should not expect him to be over patient with little chits of school-girls. *He* is an artist : poor Penn is only a man of intellect. *He* goes to the Palace three times a week ; poor Penn has only been to college ; so the two are not to be compared.

Once, however, when your dearest Kitty was making more noise over the battle of Prague than has ever been made over the battle of Waterloo, the ringleted Herr caught up her hand and said, in a voice that melted with the sweetness of barley-sugar, " I can-not perr-mit such soft litt-tle fin-gerrs to murr-derr har-mo-nie ; " and—and, dearest, I think Kitty's hand felt the smallest possible baby's-touch of a squeeze.

I had on your pretty turquoise ring at the time, and since then every girl has wished me to lend it her for her music lesson. Just as if it was the ring that ! ! !——

Fraulein Pinchinhertz is quite sentimental over the handsome Herr. She sits in the room during the lessons, looking and listening with all her soul in her eyes, and talking German in the *softest* manner. But the Herr admires his boots infinitely more than he does her.

But, bother take it, there's the bell for tea. Good-bye, my darling Nelly, and do not forget the toffee you promised to send to—   Your fondest

KITTY CLOVER.

P.S. I will show you the Valentine when I come home. Tell me have you had any ? Pray, how many ?

P.S. It is very strange—some one sang under our windows last night, " Wilt thou love me then as now ? " I wonder if it was *him* ?

P.S. I have had this more than three weeks in my pocket, waiting for an opportunity to post it.

THE EIGHTH LETTER LEFT.

(Dated April the 19th.)

SHOWING WHAT KITTY THOUGHT OF HER GOVERNESSES, AND
WHAT THE GOVERNESSES THOUGHT OF EACH OTHER.

ISN'T it strange, Nelly ?—but there doesn't appear to be a *real*
governess in the world, I mean a governess who was really
educated to be one. They are all governesses by accident.
And yet we know there are many poor girls who are brought
up young to the business, and intended for nothing else. I
wonder what becomes of them ?

All I know is, that out of all the governesses we have here,
there is only *one* who has received an education for it. That
one is Twigg. All the others have been driven into it by
necessity.

I will run through our governesses, Nell, and you shall judge
for yourself. Why, there's Blight. Her father kept his
hounds, and it seems they ran through his property in no time.
Then there's Snapp, she has danced at Almack's (so she says),
and had her lady's-maid—not an English one, but a *real
femme de chambre*, direct from Paris. Our French governess
has been just as unfortunate. She had *châteaux* innumerable
in the south of France, and domains covered with the richest
vines, olives, and truffles, only she lost them all during the
Revolution. The same with Fraulein Pinchinhertz. One half
the Danube would have been hers if it hadn't been for the
Hungarian war. And even down to poor Mrs. Dove; she would
be a rich woman if her fool of a husband hadn't taken a theatre,
and squandered all her fortune in less than a year. These
reverses are very pitiable, dear ; but I must say that, for ladies

who have been accustomed in their youth to so much wealth and luxury, they have settled down to their present drudgery with the greatest ease and the happiest contentment. I am sure if I had ever had a couple of powdered footmen standing up behind *my* carriage, that I could not have brought myself to wash and small-tooth-comb little girls in the unconcerned way they do *without a precious deal of grumbling !*

Snapp, however, does grumble a little bit when she alludes to the incident (and she is always alluding to it) of the Queen wishing her to marry a gouty old lord, who, she says, is still in search for her. My only astonishment is that he does not find her, for she goes out walking with the school every day, and takes no pains whatever in concealing herself at church.

No circulating library at the sea-side was ever so full of romance as Snapp. The mystery about her life, too, helps the romance. We know she has a hopeless attachment, for all her quotations are about "love," and she is always reading Byron, and Moore, and L. E. L. She recites beautifully. Sometimes when she comes to a very tender passage, she cries. We look upon her as the victim of an unrequited passion, and pity her, poor thing, with all our hearts.

But you must not imagine, Nelly, she is pretty. Her complexion is too much the colour of pound-cake : and her eyes are so prominent, that, when she is excited, I am afraid they will drop out of her head. She is very intellectual, for all that, and seems to know everything. It is dreadful to be examined by her. She runs a glance right through you, like a packing-needle, and can tell in a minute whether there's anything in you. When I went up before her, I felt I was going to be turned inside out, like a paper bag ; and when I left her, I came away, Nelly, with such a sense of my own emptiness, that I should like to have run away, and have hidden myself for very shame. She is certainly very clever. We are all obliged to confess it. She talks beautifully, too, about "Women's Rights ; " and the girls do say that she has in her drawers a complete *suit of the Bloomer costume*, in which she lectured one night at a neighbouring tavern, quite unknown to the Lady Principal. However, she does talk with such eloquence about the injustice of Man to Woman, that I really believe, if a proposal of marriage came to each girl at the moment she was holding forth, every one of us would indignantly refuse it !

The worst is, she is *so* very proud : she associates with no one : she considers the other governesses too much beneath her. Altogether she is much too dignified for *me*. I believe she would sooner break her back than stoop ; and that she would rather lose a marriage, by being late, than hurry herself one half-minute. None of us like Snapp ; but, as a proof how much she is dreaded and respected, not a soul in the school dares quiz her, or turn her into ridicule—excepting behind her back ! Besides, we have a notion she is some great person in disguise. The great attention, too, which she receives from Mrs. Rodwell, rather favours this impression. She invites her to supper, and sends her *tit-bits* from her own dish at dinner.

But our German and French governesses afford us rare fun. They are always bickering, always quarrelling. Mdlle. Désirée boasts about Bonaparte ; Fraulein Pinchinhertz soars into a long panegyric about Frederick the Great. Mademoiselle is singing a *chansonnette* about *la belle France ;* and the Fraulein directly begins humming something about 𝔙𝔞𝔱𝔢𝔯𝔩𝔞𝔫𝔡, or "𝔇𝔞𝔰 𝔖𝔠𝔥𝔬̈𝔫𝔢𝔰, 𝔉𝔯𝔢𝔦𝔢𝔰 𝔕𝔥𝔢𝔦𝔫." Then they are always imitating one another. If one comes down with a gay cap, the other is sure to have on the next morning a cap twenty ribbons gayer. If the hair of the one is dressed in *bandeaux* or ringlets, the hair of the other is certain, before tea-time to have fallen into *bandeaux* or ringlets also. It is the same with their bonnets, their boots, their gowns, gloves, ribbons, their everything. I believe if Mademoiselle wore Wellington boots, or went out with a gentleman's hat, that Fraulein would not be happy till she had done the same thing. They must spend all their salaries, and one-half their time, in these constant imitations of one another.

However, the German governess may work her fingers off—she may worry her ingenuity until she hasn't a rag left—it's all of no use ; she will never succeed in dressing so well as Mademoiselle Désirée ; who, though she wears only the commonest stuffs, is still the best-dressed girl in the school. Again, Fraulein has no more waist than a balloon, and yet she is always pulling herself in, until it's quite painful to look at her. Now, Mademoiselle's waist is the tiniest I ever saw. I am sure it *cannot measure* 13 *inches round*. What absurd narrowness it shows, then, on the part of Fraulein to enter into such hopeless competition ! If her body was only half as narrow as her mind, there might be a chance for her—but till then she had better save her stay-laces, and not make herself ill by drinking so much vinegar.

Fraulein is very sentimental and superstitious. She will not begin heeling a new pair of stockings on a Friday, and generally sheathes her scissors against her rival on that ominous day. She overflows with little romantic songs about water-nymphs and knights in armour, and is as full as an old nurse of supernatural legends, about witches and broomsticks, skeleton lovers, and wild hunts in the air. She raves, too, about one *Jean Paul*, whom we take to be her German lover. We love to listen at dusk, before the candles are brought in, to her tales of the Hartz mountains and her ghost stories,—so exquisitely terrible, Nelly, that we are obliged to listen to them with our eyes shut. In the midst, perhaps, the bell rings for supper, and you should hear us all shriek again with fear ! As soon as she has finished, Mademoiselle begins quizzing, and spoils the effect by turning everything she has said into fun. Then she rattles off with some lively anecdote, which chases the ghosts away better than any holy water, and only excites contempt of the most *sauerkrout* sourness in the mind of Fraulein for French frivolity.

I reserve Twigg for a future letter. I want to tell you now about poor Mrs. Dove. We have many girls studying with us to be governesses—practising for a future life of martyrdom. Mrs. Dove is one of these pupil-slaves. She is so pretty, so gentle, Nelly, so interesting, that all the school loves her and pities her ; not that we ever rudely express our pity, for I often think that, to a sensitive mind, pity is only another kind of alms-giving, and that a poor person will turn from it with the same wounded delicacy as if you tendered charity. I may be wrong, Nelly; but, never mind. Our pity to Mrs. Dove is of that silent kind that only expresses itself in little acts of kindness, which she receives as silently, but, I am sure, not the less gratefully.

Poor creature ! she is sadly in need of kindness, for she is a *widow ! a real widow*, Nelly, all alone in this world (for her husband, after he had squandered her fortune, shot himself in remorse) ; but no, not all alone, for she has *her baby with her —such a darling baby !* which she clings to as a drowning person clings to the plank that is his last support. It is such a beautiful little dear ! Can't you conceive the life of a baby in a boarding-school, Nell ? Any baby, let it be ever so ugly, would be prized, and made much of ; but, when it is such a lovely little angel as this, you can have no conception how it is petted and caressed ; how we almost fight to get hold of it, and how, having got hold of it, we are ready to fight again before we part with it. I wonder he has not been pulled, like a doll, into a thousand pieces, in our numerous struggles to obtain possession of him, and nurse him, if it is only for two or three minutes. I wonder all his senses have not been tossed, like so much bran, out of him as we have amused ourselves for hours in tossing him up to the ceiling and catching him again in our arms, raising quite a cackling chorus of "chick-achick-a-biddies " all the while. I wonder he has not been poisoned long ago, with the numerous sweeties and many-coloured goodies we have stuffed down his little throat ; and, lastly, I wonder more than all, what with his mother kissing

him, and what with all of us kissing him from morning to
night, that the little fellow has not been regularly *kissed to
death* by this time.   He is only eighteen months old now ; but
if he ever knows happiness hereafter, what he at present enjoys
should be sufficient to last him all his life.   What a pity it is
he cannot remain as he is.   What a happy existence, to be
perpetually a baby in a girls' school !   I cannot imagine anything more delicious out of Paradise, Nell !   Perpetual inno-
cence, love, play, and enjoyment ! with no cares, no troubles,
no pain, except from being a little overfed occasionally.

Mrs. Dove is no party to our romps.   She has no heart for
it.   It would not look natural with the deep seams of grief upon
her face.   She never smiles, excepting when she is alone with
her boy and attempts to play with him ; and then it is a
smile that begs for pity as seen through her widow's cap—
the smile of one who was smiling through the bars of a prison.
She is never away from her books.   Her melancholy never seems
at rest, excepting when she is studying ; and I am sure she must
have a constant headache from excess of it.   From morning to
midnight, she never pauses ; never goes out to allow a few rays
of sunshine to enter into the dark despondency of her breast; but
you will always find her in some lonely corner, learning, learning,
learning, until it is pitiable to see how deadly pale she looks,
and horrible to reflect how long so severe a trial of the mind
and body can last.   She scarcely allows herself a few moments
for baby even ; denying herself the luxury of its caresses,
tearing herself away from its chubby little arms, and resigning
him to the affection of a stranger, to begin again the endless
task, the task which seems to engross all her faculties and
energy—the task whose only end can be to leave the child
without a mother.

We think she has no friends, and is without means, and that
she is slaving herself in this way to maintain her child as a
governess, but it's ridiculous, Nelly, *she* will never make a
governess ; with her lady-like manners—her saint-like sweet-

ness—her angelic forbearance ; so humble, so patient and enduring, so modest and doubtful of her own abilities ! She may break her heart in the effort ; she may turn all her virtues into as many vices; and even then what chance has she against that she-dragon Snapp, with a mouth filled with wise teeth, and an old maid's tongue tipped with poison ?

We know nothing of her story, and even that sneaking Carney has paused, as before a sanctuary, in the presence of such holy grief, and has not dared to ask a single question as to the secret of so many tears. But it is clear, Nelly, the poor widow *is here cheap.* We know that plainly enough from the Lady Principal's laying such stress on the obligation of receiving a baby into the school, and a regular splutter of twaddle about her benevolence and generosity, which was worse than crossing the Channel to listen to. Besides Mrs. Dove never goes into supper with the other governesses, but has a bit of dry bread, like the girls ; and she has to wait on herself, sleeping in a dark little closet, where the wonder is how she can see to kiss baby, much less to dress the dear little fellow !

Poor mother ! I hope she may never be taunted, nor teased, nor bullied, nor snubbed, as most governesses are ; but that she may always be treated with the gentleness of her own nature ; and that each tear she drops into the cup of life may sweeten the bitter draught for her !

Good night, Nelly. After this little history I am sure you cannot wish to hear anything more at present from

Your loving, sleepy-eyed

KITTY CLOVER.

P.S. Twigg (she is the niece of the Lady Principal, and is also studying for a governess, for she is destined some day to walk into her aunt's educational shoes, but then she is studying in a very different way to poor Mrs. Dove!) has promised to drop this in the post for me on condition I get her a portrait of my brother Oscar, and a lock of his hair.

P. S. Bother take it ! to-morrow is washing night.

THE NINTH LETTER LEFT.

(*Dated May 1st.*)

SHOWING WHAT TOOK PLACE AT SCHOOL ON A MOST
IMPORTANT OCCASION.

THERE is no school to-day, Nelly. We have got a holiday, and I mean to enjoy it by writing to you, dearest.

My pretty Eleanor must know that it has been our *confirmation morning*. At last they are all off; and it has been such a busy time of crying and laughing—of such frivolity one moment, and hysterical excitement the next—that I am not sorry they are gone. I thought they never would be ready! The fuss began as early as six o'clock. First of all the clergyman came—then the hair-dresser (though he styles himself on his cards " *artiste en cheveux* ")—then a breathless milliner—then a puffing shoemaker—then more milliners and more shoemakers—so that really it has been nothing but *hurry, flurry, worry, skurry*, ever since we opened our eyes this morning. The door knocker has been going incessantly for four hours—and there seemed to be a competition between it and the girls' tongues as to which of the two should make the greatest noise. So if my letter throbs with a slight headache, Nell, you will know exactly on whose head to lay the fault.

To begin, Lizzy's dress was too short, and Jessie's was so long that it might have run an express train (Meggy Sharpe said) all the way to Brentford! More than this, the two Suetts could not get their frocks to meet, and it was laughable to see them running about, begging of every one to help to lace them. No one's dress seemed to fit, excepting Amy

Darling's ; but I believe if Amy was to try on a barrister's
silk gown, that by some miracle it would fit her as beautifully
as the dresses in a French fashion book !

Poor Mary Owen seemed in a dream. It made me unhappy
to notice her. She was dressed in an ugly, thick, bed-gowny
garment, which was thought "quite good enough for her."
Her cheeks were transparently pale. Her large eyes, so full
of sorrow, were lit up with a strange radiance as if a light
was burning behind them. It put me in mind of the light I
have sometimes seen burning over a tomb; and as I saw
Mary's lips move as if in silent prayer, the picture of a tomb
in some gloomy vault, with the dark figure of a woman
stretched over it, rose without my helping it before my
imagination. I thought Mary was the mourner, and the
tomb was the one in which were buried all her hopes of
happiness in this world.

A warm colour flushed over the poor girl's face (like the tint
of a cathedral window falling on some marble statue), when she
first noticed the difference between her shroud-like frock and
the gay dresses of her companions ; but it quickly passed
away, *like a bad thought one's been ashamed to think of.*
After she had assisted to dress Amy, she was going to put on
the ugly thing, when Amy pushed it aside and brought forth
one just like her own, made by the *same dressmaker* out of
the *same materials,* and sent by her mamma for " dear Mary."

Then, Nelly, poor Owen was quite overcome—weeping,
reproaching, and caressing Amy by turns—saying first " it
was too bad of her," and then that " it was too good of her,"
and hanging round her neck, as if she was the only one dear
object on earth she had to cling to—and doing it all so
touchingly that in less time than you can put on your bonnet
we were all crying, and I firmly believe (so contagious is
goodness, Nelly,) that every girl present was angry with
herself that she had not done the same thing, and wished in
atonement to pull off her beautiful dress, and offer it to Mary.

This crying took so long that there would not have been a piece of dry muslin carried to church that day, if the Lady Principal had not come up stairs to inquire into the reason of the delay. There she found the *artiste* tearing his hair (after the old approved French recipe for *désespoir*) in such a liberal manner as to soon require the use of one of his own wigs; there she heard the governesses exhausted with scolding; there she saw the girls with red eyes and " *rats' tails* " that " would be a disgrace to any school." Oh, dear! oh, dear! what a storm there was after our little shower!

It was a lovely sight, Nelly, these twelve young girls in pure white, with their long lace veils—many of them pretty enough for brides—and all of them beautified for the occasion, although, except with Mary and Amy, I do not think there *was much thought of religion.* It seemed to me that their thoughts were all wrapt up in their fine clothes.

Carney was the only ugly one, sneaking and prying behind her veil, as if it could conceal from heavenly eyes her want of truthfulness. And those proud creatures—Noble and Peacock! May I always be as poor as one of our Saturday's dinners, if they hadn't got *Honiton veils* and *white bouquets* to *distinguish them from the rest!* On an occasion like the present I think they might have kept their pride in their drawers at home— *n'est-ce-pas*, Nelly?

Just as they were starting, the Lady Principal came into the room to address " a few words of motherly admonition to her dear children." She had scarcely got half-way through her first sentence of big words—every one of which rolled along as heavily as an omnibus on a breaking-up day—when she espied Mary's graceful appearance. She grew crimson at the sight, and, calling her forward, inquired, in a voice as ragged and as cutting as a saw, " Pray, Miss Owen, inform me why you have presumed to wear other than the costume I considered suited to your *position.* What new pride, I should like to know, is this, my fine young lady? "

Before Mary could stammer out a word Amy had darted forward, and was "telling the whole tale." The dress had arrived too late to consult the Lady Principal; she was very sorry it had not been done: if it was any one's fault it was hers; and she begged that the punishment might not be visited upon any one else, but upon her alone. As the noble girl spoke, the white veil round her head shone like a bright fleecy cloud, and her voice sounded in my ears like an angel's that was speaking out of it.

There was no time for lecturing, or the indulgence of spite, or revenge, or else I am sure Mary would have had, after all, to wear the white smock; and as for Amy, I tremble, dear, like a dish of blancmange, to think what tortures might have been in store for her!

Well, after pivoting them round and round to see that all was tidy, and everybody running to fetch something that had been forgotten, the chosen twelve were pronounced "ready," and divided into two parties, six for each yellow fly.

At this point, Mrs. Dove made her appearance in the room. Her eyes were swollen, as though she had only just left off crying. She was dressed in the deepest mourning, and as she pressed her baby boy to her bosom, she looked a sad picture of woman's acutest suffering. There was something so solemn, so pathetic in the contrast of her dark widowhood amongst these youthful bridal figures, that awe stopped every tongue, and we suddenly stood still, looking pitifully on her grief, and for the moment becoming sharers in it. She did not say a word, but somehow her sorrow spoke to us with the eloquence of a touching sermon. Each step, each look, was a heart-rending appeal to our sympathies; to gaze upon her was to feel filled with charity. I daren't look round, but I am sure there wasn't a dry eye in the room.

She placed the sleeping infant in Blight's arms, and joined the party that was going to church; for it seems that, though

married, she had never been confirmed, and that she had
secretly prepared for the ceremony.

Poor struggling widow !   There at least was faith and hope,
for without them what would her life be worth ?   No finery—
no Honiton laces—no love of show had urged her to her present
act—no tender exhortations of a young and handsome clergyman had prepared her spirit, and yet, Mary dear, from my
heart I prayed that, when I was confirmed, it might be as
she was—in *humble religious sincerity* and *my common every-
day dress.*

Oh ! there they are back.   I must run to hear all about it.
Excuse this abrupt flight of

Yours, Nelly love,

The same as ever,

KITTY.

P.S. The Lady Principal is delighted.   The Reverend Mr.
Meltam (his hair is parted *so* beautifully down the middle,
dear,) complimented her upon the " extremely good behaviour
of her pupils." · The whole twelve, and Mrs. Dove too, are
invited to take supper with her this evening.

P.S. I don't mind telling *you*, Nelly, we are going to have
a supper to-night ; not a common supper with the governesses
—off stale sandwiches and small beer—but a *snug little supper
up stairs in our own bedroom*—sweets smuggled in a fright,
and eaten in a tremble.   The excitement is the best part of it,
though I must confess justice is generally done to the sausage-
rolls, the banbury-puffs, and the other dainties provided.   We
wait until Blight has gone her visiting rounds.   When everything is quiet, Lucy Wilde or Rosy Mary begins telling some
horrible story, often reciting an entire novel in a quarter of an
hour.   As soon as we are sure all spies are asleep, and that
there's not even a mouse stirring, the wax-ends, stuck into
pomatum pots, are lighted (unless the moon graciously gives us
the light of her countenance), and the feasting begins.   There

are only six girls in our room—Wilde, Mary, Sharpe, St. Ledger, Embden, and my worthy self. Fraulein sleeps in a little closet, about as big as a china-cupboard, called a dressing-room; but she is a good hard sleeper, and never wakes or hears anything of our midnight revels. Once, however, I thought I heard her giggling under the bedclothes, when Sharpe was telling a frightful German tragedy. Perhaps she was enjoying the fun quietly by herself, though why she should laugh, when every one else was shivering with fear over the frightful love incidents, is more than I can tell. Well, Nelly, the banquet is spread on one of the girl's beds, round which we all sit, somewhat in tailor-fashion. There is not much variety in our entertainments, as we can only send to the confectioners; but it does not matter. If we had roasted peacocks, or sweetmeats prepared by nuns, or all the rich things in the Lord Mayor's larder, we could not enjoy them more. It is such rare fun, and worth any of the grand dinners you go to, Nelly. Sometimes an alarm is given, and, quicker than any conjuror's trick, the wax-ends are extinguished, the goodies disappear no one knows where, and in less than a minute *every one is fast asleep*. It's very strange, but Blight, call as loud as she will, *never can wake us*. This trick, however, is sometimes sadly annoying. The rapidity of the change crumbles the light pastry all into nothing, and in the quickness of the transformation one cannot always recollect *whose turn it is to be helped next*. Besides, there is the danger, as you jump into bed in the dark, of falling upon half-a-dozen "turnovers," which, in the hurry of the surprise, have been swept in between your sheets to get them out of the way. On one occasion I saw St. Ledger smeared all over with jam, until she looked like a large "rolly-polly pudding." How we did laugh to be sure! As our suppers are *rather rich*, we generally have a little *eau de Cologne* sprinkled on a lump of sugar—just sufficient to scare away the nightmare—though we prefer the essence of peppermint (when we can get it) mixed

with a little water.   You can't think how nice and warming it
is !   To night Embden has got a cucumber and some maids-
of-honour, and we expect a rare treat.   By-the-by, Nelly,
when you come and see me, remember our supper-table.
Bring something sweet and rich with you, and put into your
pocket some wax-ends.   Our stock of chandlery is rather low
at present.   Come soon, there's a dear pet.

THE TENTH LETTER LEFT.

(*Dated May the* 16*th.*)

SHOWING WHO WAS THE THIEF.

IN my last letter, Nelly, I alluded to a tea party.   As you
can have no idea what such an entertainment can be like,
I will describe one for you.

The seniors only are admitted.   One must have numbered
fifteen blushing summers, and have attained the altitude of the
first degree, before being entitled to this great honour.   One
by one we are announced, and received, introduced, and seated
as at a formal party.   Each young lady plays in her turn the
hostess, and tries her best to entertain her guests.   She is the
goddess of the tea-tray, and has absolute control over the thin
bread and butter (what a shadowy mockery to *hungry school
girls*, each of whom could devour an entire loaf !).   But we
would not mind being put on short commons, if we were not
compelled to talk.   *That* is the greatest cruelty.   Every young
lady is expected to *bring a new idea.*   You may laugh at this,
Miss Nelly, and fancy we are not so cruelly treated after all,
but let me tell you that new ideas are not so easily caught
as a cold.   I have known poor girls lie awake for nights, and
yet not succeed in finding one.   Just you try to get a new idea
every day of your life, and see how soon you'll break down !

Our new ideas are ushered into conversation in the following manner :—

Lizzy Spree. " It is remarkable that balloons were invented in the year 1755—the same year that George the Second reigned on the throne of England."

(A dead silence, and another cup of tea handed round.)

Susan Carney. " If we could only see ourselves with the eyes of other people, we should examine the faults of ourselves more, and the faults of others less ! "

(A long pause to recover from this withering sarcasm.)

Meggy Sharpe. " It is a most curious fact, but at the same time no less true, that the tortoise, which provides us with the beautiful shell for our combs, has not the smallest particle of hair itself."

Emilia Suett. " The introduction of pine-apples from the West Indies took place in the year 1845, and since then have become so plentiful that they are not unfrequently sold in the streets for a penny a slice."

I forgot to tell you that Miss Priscilla Hextra (Mrs. Rodwell's maiden sister) is the Queen who receives us, every evening, on these state occasions. After each *new idea*, she delivers a short lecture, made doubly wise, by being delivered through a pair of green spectacles. She corrects us when wrong, compliments us when we are right, and in every case says " a few words relevant to the subject in question." For instance, with regard to pine-apples, she told us about the culture of them, informed us of their former price, inveighed against the alarming increase of luxuries, compared the extravagance of modern London with the abstinence of ancient Sparta, and so arrived at the conclusion that black broth was infinitely better for the health, both physical and moral, of a nation, than turtle-soup !

At last the half-hour strikes, we take a ceremonious leave, and escape down stairs to coax Susan for the remains of the *thick* bread and butter.

Now, Nelly, I dare say these invitations are meant kindly

enough, but what possible good do they do us ? We are too
frightened to talk, and as for enjoying ourselves, we are sitting all
the while upon pins and needles thinking of our "new idea." The
notion, moreover, that it teaches us how to receive company is
absurd ! Goodness forbid, that I should ever play the part of
hostess to my friends in the same chilly, ceremonious, manner
my nervousness makes me display on these solemn occasions.
Besides, it's rather cruel to school us, when school is over,
under the pretence of hospitality !

We have had such a merry time of it, lately !—such lots of
half-holidays. Last week, too, was the Race Week. You should
have seen how well our school turned out. We were all dressed
in our Sunday best, and mistresses, half-boarders, the Lady
Principal, and even her sister Priscilla, all joined in the ranks
to make the procession look longer. It was quite a grand sight.
The tall girls were placed first—and they gradually grew less
and less in size till the shortest came last—something like the
shape of the Pandean pipes. Mrs. Spankit's school passed
us in the High Street. They looked a mere apron-string by
the side of our long line, and they wisely disappeared down
the first street. The best thing after a defeat is to run away.
No wonder the gentlemen, returning home from the races, took
such notice of us ! They kissed their hands, threw bouquets,
and pelted us with nuts, pincushions, and motto bonbons. My
pocket was as full of kisses as a baby's face. I caught a pear,
a set of wooden tea-things inside, notwithstanding Snapp's
rage, who thought it was *meant for her*. I never knew such
conceit. But this fun was too good to last. After a time
Mrs. Rodwell got very indignant, and took us home by the
back-lanes.

There was such a to-do when we returned to the Princesses'
College. The whole school was assembled, and, after a severe
lecture, ten of the eldest girls were condemned to " *Silenzia*."
This is a dreadful punishment, Nelly—the severest we have—
and is a million times worse than solitary confinement. *You*

are struck dumb all at once. You are not allowed to say a word—not even to talk to yourself—and if any girl speaks to you, or you are seen speaking to any girl, she is *silenced* also ; and so, in self-defence, no one will let you say a word.

Once the whole College was *silenced in this way for a fortnight.* It was so curious ! A stranger, coming in, would have fancied it were a Deaf and Dumb Asylum, or that he was visiting by mistake a *Seminary for Young Quakeresses.* You imagine, perhaps, we were very miserable. Not a bit of it ! We never had more fun, for somehow a school girl will extract fun out of almost everything. We talked with our fingers—we kept up conversations on our slates—we expressed our opinions by means of pantomime (how you would have laughed to have seen Lucy Wilde play the balcony scene in *Romeo and Juliet* without saying a word !), we corresponded on slips of paper, until there was so much noise, such continued tittering, such loud explosions of laughter, that the Lady Principal was glad to give us the use of our tongues again. The loss of it makes a woman desperate. I must say I never felt so truly wicked as when I was sentenced to this unnatural dumbness. Speech relieves the heart of many an evil thought. Besides, this silent system encourages *sulking,* and only see how bad sulky people generally are. Then, again, I want to know, if it is made a crime to speak, how are we to say our prayers ?

I was looking out for you, Nelly, all the afternoon on the Horticultural Fête Day. We had another half-holiday. We were allowed as a great favour to walk in the front garden ; but, only after we had put on our dancing dresses. Mary Owen was excluded ; her bonnet was not " good enough." All the windows were thrown open, ·by chance, of course, and not done purposely to show the rows of white dimity beds, and the drawings, maps, and large globes ; and, doubtlessly, it was by accident also, that Annie Flower was kept playing all day in the drawing-room with the *loud-pedal down* (she is one of our best players, only the noise she makes gives you the head-ache

sometimes). It is very wrong to notice these things, but
school-girls have got nothing else to do. In the same way, we
couldn't help noticing that the Lady Principal was seated near
the window, all the time the carriages were rattling by, dressed in
the most elegant *déshabille*, and with a most elegant book and
cambric handkerchief in her hand. She doesn't read so much
on other days ! However, we had plenty of amusement, though
those tiresome boys next door nearly frightened us out of our
lives by throwing over detonating balls, and by firing off little
cannons every other minute.

Oh ! such a dreadful thing has occurred. For a whole week
nothing else has been talked of. You must know, dearest
Nelly, that for some time past *a number of things have been
disappearing.* Crochet-needles, pencil-cases, scissors, pen-
knives, all vanished, and no one could tell how, or when, or
where. The number of handkerchiefs that were missing
would suffice a whole theatre any night Mr. Charles Kean was
playing. Nothing was safe, and one evening when I went up
to bed I found that my night-gown had gone also. I was
so put out, you can't tell. Well, the servants were accused
the first, and they were dismissed ; but as the same mysterious
disappearance went on just as mysteriously as before, it was
clear it couldn't be them. No girl liked to accuse another ;
but it was perfectly evident, as Snapp said, that *the things
couldn't walk off without hands.* I never saw the Lady
Principal so upset, and well she might, for if the objects had
only kept flying away with the same miraculous rapidity, there
wouldn't have been by this time a single thing left in the
school. She didn't know whom to accuse. However, as " an
example " was wanted, poor Mary Owen was punished each
time for the thief, although we all knew Mary would not *take
a lump of sugar* that wasn't her own.

Well, last Tuesday, Noble's guardian came with his grand
phaeton, and gave her a sovereign. Out of pride she stuck it
on her desk, that every one might see it. In a little time *it*

was gone! No one could tell how, or had noticed any one take it; *but it was gone!*

What a *fuss* ensued! The room was swept; the desk and drawers were turned inside out; all our pockets were searched: but no sovereign could be found. It was very singular. The Lady Principal appealed to us, and spoke beautifully about the sin of stealing. She entreated the culprit to confess—promised forgiveness—and gave us each a piece of paper of the same size, on which we were to write, " *I am* " or " *I am not* the thief," that *she alone* might know the sinner.

The papers were handed in, opened, and, as you may guess, *were all alike.* Every girl had written down, " *I am not the thief.* "

Then, amidst a silence such as I have never heard before, and with all our cheeks burning, the Lady Principal gave us a long lecture; and concluded by saying that in her mind she had not the slightest doubt Mary Owen was the culprit—she was the only vicious, evil-minded girl in the College—too hardened in crime even to acknowledge her fault.

Poor Mary protested, with her tears and her blushes, that she was innocent of the base charge; but the more she protested, the louder grew the reproaches upon her wickedness. She was locked up in the cloak-cupboard, where you can hardly tell whether it is night or day, and allowed nothing but bread and water. Day after day, *for nearly a week*, she was visited by Mrs. Rodwell, who tried every persuasion and every threat to induce her to confess; but all in vain. Mary simply said, " I have nothing to confess."

Amy Darling cried herself ill over her friend's disgrace, and scarcely slept for watching, in order to discover who was the real thief.

Now listen, dear Nelly, with all your eyes and ears, to the story how Amy's sisterly vigilance was rewarded. Last Friday a large hamper came for the two Suetts: it contained

Indian preserves and pickles, and cakes, and fruit, and *all sorts of good things*. As we had to go out walking, the hamper was only just peeped into, and left, with the lid open, in the school-room. Amy, who really had made herself unwell, was allowed to stop at home and lie on the sofa; but I believe her object more particularly was to visit Mary Owen *on the sly*, and comfort her in her dreary place of confinement.

When we returned home, the school-room was locked, and the key removed. The servants were sent for; they knew nothing about it. Amy was summoned, and, taking the key from her pocket, opened the door, saying, "There, Mrs. Rodwell, there is the thief."

True enough, there was Carney lying on the ground, with jars, half-empty, strewed about her, and the hamper upset, and its delicious contents littered about the room. She was crying, and seemed to be very miserable and ill. She rose, however, and, moaning most piteously, fell upon her knees, looking so conscience-stricken, that, guilty as she was, I half-pitied her.

Amy, upon being questioned, explained, how lying upon the sofa she had heard the school-room door open. Knowing no one was in the house but herself and the servants, she crept cautiously down stairs to spy and to *reconnoitre*. To her astonishment she discovered the sneaking Carney, who had returned home from the walk upon some slight excuse, helping herself most liberally to the rich things in the Suetts' hamper. She was eating away as if it was her last meal, and filling her pockets at the same time to lay in a good store for the next. Amy said nothing, but, gently closing the door, turned the key upon her.

Oh, Nelly! what a scene followed! Carney, seeing there was no hope of mercy, flung herself upon the floor, and crawled and writhed like a serpent. Some kind friend had rushed out instantly, and liberated poor Mary Owen. She came into the room, looking as pale as death, and her whole frame trembling. Instinctively, as it were, she ran to Amy, for her heart seemed to lead her to her as naturally as a child goes to its mother, and she must have fallen, if the dear angel (*for she is an angel*, truly,) had not caught her in her arms. Then the Lady Principal went up to her with a gentleness I had never seen in her before, and taking hold of Mary's hand, raised it to her lips. She spoke, but her tones were so full of kindness that I should not have known it for the same voice. " My dear Miss Owen," she said, " I have been harsh and unjust. I have come to ask you to have the grace to forgive me. I am painfully sorry for what I have done." Mary summoned all her strength, and rose from her chair. She attempted to speak, but tears flowed instead of words, and, sobbing as if her heart must break, she threw herself round her mistress's neck and kissed her. I don't recollect anything more.

The same evening Mary found a parcel under her pillow. It was a beautiful edition of the Bible, with a dear inscription in the *Lady Principal's own hand-writing*. You've no idea how proud the poor girl is of it.

Good bye, my dear pet Nelly. I have written till I am quite unhappy. Kiss me, and let me close this stupid letter.

KITTY.

P.S. It is Mrs. Rodwell's birthday next Monday week. It is usual to give her a present on that occasion. Every girl contributes what she can afford, and sometimes more than she can afford, in order to *curry favour*. It is not generally an offering of the heart, Nelly. Most girls give because they daren't refuse ; but this year every purse has been emptied, and I doubt if there is a penny left in the school to give to a beggar. This is only the first collection ; but it's very strange, the Lady Principal has suddenly become quite popular.

P.S. Oh! I had nearly forgotten to tell you, that half-an-hour after the above discovery, a fly came round to the door. Carney's boxes were placed in it, and, after restoring to each girl what she had taken, and humbly begging their pardon, she was sent home with Snapp, *disgraced* and *expelled*.

Do you know my night-gown was found in her box ? I wasn't so angry with her as I expected I should be ; but told her " she might keep it if she wished." She looked at me so sorrowfully : but good-bye.

THE ELEVENTH LETTER LEFT.

(Dated May 29th and June 1st.)

SHOWING UP A TERRIBLE ABUSE, AND A FRIGHTFUL MYSTERY.

YESTERDAY was a half-holiday, and we had all been busy helping Amy Darling in making a plum-cake for little Jessie Joy's birthday. Twigg bought the plums, sugar, and spice. Susan got us the flour, butter, and eggs—and Embden *mixed it in a washing-basin* (don't faint, Nelly, as I should have done at one time : there is no place like school for curing a person of daintiness). The cake looks remarkably nice, and cook has promised to bake it (for a shilling). It is as full as it can hold of large pieces of candied lemon-peel, and I am looking forward to the agreeable surprise it will be to our pretty Jessie.

After washing the paste from my fingers, as I intended having half an hour's practice, I was going leisurely down to the drawing-room, when up rushed a tall red-faced man, *all hair and moustaches.* He seized hold of me, and before I could remember to scream, kissed me two or three times. Oh! dear, Nelly, I was so frightened that I quite forgot to box his ears, and it was as much as I could do to run upstairs and lock myself in the first bed-room, where I seized hold of the pitcher, and was prepared to throw its contents over the first person that came in. Accidentally I caught a peep of my face

in the glass, and I *looked such a fright* that I shouldn't have
known myself again.

Well, Nelly, as soon as the stairs were clear, I ran down to
tell all about this long-haired monster (I am sure he could be
no gentleman—he smelt so terribly of tobacco). I found the
whole school in a fearful state of consternation. It seems he had
walked into the middle of the room with his hands in his pockets,
and then walked out again *whistling*—but not before he had
patted Annie Flower and Noble under the chin with his filthy,
dirty hands, *with no gloves on.* I told my little adventure,
when suddenly we heard a loud noise above, and *then a piercing
scream*, which made us all jump. Snapp and Blight, and
every one of the mistresses ran out of the room, and *left us
quite alone.*

How quiet the school was that afternoon ! We forgot everything about our cake in the intensity of the excitement.
Every girl seemed afraid to speak. If we quarrelled, our
highest words went no higher than a whisper. All our games
were dropped. The noisiest *romps* walked about on tiptoe. The
grand-piano was closed. Every door leading to the upper part
of the college was locked. Orders were given that no one was
to leave the school-room under any pretence whatever. A deep
silence moaned throughout the house, like a person breathing
heavily in his sleep. Even the school-mistresses talked low, as
if there was a *friend dangerously ill in the room*,—and the
girls, as they were broken into small groups, with their heads
huddled close together, looked like physicians consulting
anxiously on the patient's case. In the midst of the obscurity,
too, dark rumours went floating about, like shadows, increasing
every one's fears, until it was quite a relief when *the candles
were brought in.* It was a sad evening—a painful half-holiday,
Nelly ; not a bit of supper was eaten ; Miss Priscilla did not
hold her usual tea-party ; and the only "*new idea* " discussed
—and that in corners, amongst ourselves—was the grand mystery as to who this big-whiskered stranger could be ? About

eight o'clock we flitted noiselessly up to bed,—not a board creaked, and, instead of a set of noisy school-girls, you would have taken us for *a flight of ghosts gliding about a haunted house.*

As we passed the Lady Principal's private room, we held our breaths. If we had been going through a churchyard, at twelve o'clock at night, we could not have been more quiet, or more frightened. We listened, but did not hear a sound, *not a groan.* Meggy Sharpe tried to *look through the key-hole,* but was pulled away by the German mistress, who seemed to look upon it as something worse than a Chamber of Horrors.

That same night none of us slept. We talked softly—and each girl vowed she would write home the next day, and tell her parents of the shameful goings-on. We all agreed it was scandalous, and the prospect of an immediate liberation from the college made us secretly rejoice rather at what had occurred.

Meggy Sharpe got so restless at last, that she jumped out of bed, and listened at the door. The foolish girl must have caught her death of cold, for she stopped shivering there, though kept warm by her curiosity and the counterpane she had wrapped around her, for more than half an hour. All of a sudden, she cried " Hush." The *boudoir* door had opened. She hung over the banisters as far as she could, and there, inside the room, she saw the same monster, *lying at full length with his muddy boots on the yellow damask sofa.* He was *puffing a cigar,* and in his hand he held a glass of what looked very much like *cold brandy-and-water.* By this time all the girls in our bed-room had jumped out of bed, and were peeping over the bannisters as well. We saw the Lady Principal sitting by this wretch's side—with her handkerchief up to her eyes— and the tears running from her *like water from a bathing-woman.* Miss Priscilla was there too, looking as white as a pinafore, and spilling the lavender drops she was trying to mix for her sister. There was not one amongst us, I am sure, but who felt sincerely for their sufferings, for, whether it was with the cold or the excitement, I know we all kept trembling and shaking together, like I have seen *the drops on a chandelier during a delicious polka.*

We listened, and, in broken bits, we heard him say, as he alternately puffed and then said a few words, blowing them out drawlingly like so much smoke, " Come, now, no nonsense, old woman (the idea of calling the Lady Principal an 'old woman!') I've had a run of luck against me—I tell you I *must have a cool hundred*—or else, by Jove—I'll send for my traps, and stop here, till you haven't a young chick left out of your whole brood,"—and then he smoked like a chimney on Christmas-Day.

What the above meant I did not half understand, but just at the above point, his nasty, filthy tobacco-smoke got down my throat and made me cough. The sound startled Miss Priscilla, who, discovering the door was open, very quickly shut it.

The next morning he was gone before we were up, but on the staircase I found a piece of pasteboard on which was written " 50 *to* 1 *against The Devil-amongst-the-Tailors.*" Meggy says it is a betting-ticket.

Well now, Nelly, who do you think this mysterious monster is ? I might give you ten thousand, and you would never guess it. Why, dear, it was *Mr. Rodwell!* no less a person than *Mrs. Rodwell's own husband!* who we all thought had been killed in the Sikh campaign, and buried years ago in Westminster Abbey. We found it out by his name being on the above ticket. Lor ! how surprised I was when I heard it ; if our handsome music-master had made me a proposal of marriage, I could not have felt more startled. Imagine the Lady Principal having a lord and master to rule *her*—she who rules us all, isn't it strange ? I should as soon have thought of the sun being split in two as her individuality being divided ! I can no more conceive her proud majestic spirit being under the command of another person, any more than I can conceive the Queen of England being told by a policeman to " move on."

We have only seen the Lady Principal once since. Her eyes were swollen, and she spoke meekly, as if she had just risen from a bed of sickness. She remitted several fines, and kissed two or three of us before leaving the room. Poor woman! I pity her with all my heart. I'm sure it's wrong of us to augment her sorrows, when she has so many of her own. I, for one, will try all I can for the future to please her.

Susan has this moment run out to fetch the doctor. Dear Mrs. Rodwell has been carried to bed in the most violent hysterics. We all feel inclined to cry. Amy Darling has been speaking to us in her usual kind manner, and says we must not think of writing home a word about what has occurred. It's to be a secret amongst ourselves, and we have all vowed to keep it, and I am confident not a girl will break it. So, dearest Nelly, you mustn't say a word about this to any one.

What do you think, Nelly—*he's* a gambler. It seems that so long as he wins he does not *bother* Mrs. Rodwell much, but as soon as he loses (and he's always losing) he comes and bullies her, and will not leave the house till he's got the money he wants. On one occasion when she hadn't any—she had given him every farthing—he brought a party of six Polish noblemen (so he called them) to the house, and said he wanted to put them to school to have them properly "finished" (I'd have soon finished them *by scratching their eyes out*) ; and on another occasion, when she hadn't anything to give him, he *carried off all her jewels*, and a *beautiful silver teapot* besides, which we had given her on her birthday. Just as if we subscribed our pocket-money to buy *him* presents! Isn't it enough, dear, to make you turn a nun when you hear of such *brutes of husbands* as that?—but mind, darling, mum, not a word.

*　　　*　　　*　　　*　　　*

I have opened my letter, Nelly, dearest, as Twigg (who has been my postmistress lately) has had the mumps, and Susan has grown over-nice and particular, though I did offer her

sixpence and a pair of 'my best gloves to slip this in the post
for me.

Fraulein has been making us all love her to-day. During
play-hours, she was requested to attend the Lady Principal in
her *"boudoir."* We all thought it was for a reprimand—but
no ! in two or three minutes she returned, her face crimson,
her eyes sparkling, and began dancing about the room, clapping her hands all the while, and jabbering German till we
made sure the girl had gone crazy. As soon as she was tired
of this mad game, she snatched a little parcel from her bosom,
and smothered it in kisses, declaiming, laughing, and dancing
all at the same time. Then suddenly she undid the paper, and
spread out four sovereigns in a row, taking up them to kiss
fervently again and again, as if they were friends that were
going on a long journey.

Snapp, who had been looking on in dignified contempt, at
last burst out, " Really, Fraulein, I can no longer permit this
weak display of mercenary feelings. If you cannot command
your covetous exultation (Snapp is dearly fond of long words),
it would be more judicious of you to *retire,* so that your
example may not have an injurious effect on the disinterested
purity of youth." " Or," she continued, finding her words
quite unheeded, " if your parents are in such necessitous circumstances, I have no doubt the young ladies will subscribe
something for their relief, and I shall be happy to contribute
a trifle myself towards the *charity.*"

These words fell like a blow upon Fraulein in the midst of
her joy. Feeling herself cruelly wounded, she flew at Snapp,
and talked German so fast, that we expected to see the teeth
flying out of her head every minute. How it might have ended,
I cannot say, if Mademoiselle and Blight had not interfered.
Fraulein allowed Blight to lead her quietly to the other end of
the room, where she fell into a chair, and began crying like a
child. We formed in a circle round her, and this is what we
learnt to be the cause of her joy and grief.

It seems poor, good-natured Fraulein had been plodding, fagging, and whipping our lazy brains *for a period of two years, and all for nothing !* Isn't it wretched? *Isn't it most cruel,* Nelly? to pay (or rather not to pay at all) women at this rate ; but it would appear it is the inevitable condition of the drudgery of a poor governess's life ! Let us hope, dear girl, no reverse in life will ever reduce us to the same hard fate; though the knowledge of the fact should teach us to treat the poor outcast creatures with greater kindness, as I am certain we should all have done, if we had only known it, in the instance of dear, patient, good-humoured Fraulein. It is curious the amount of suffering many souls can endure without complaining ! Imagine this good German girl, away from home—away from all her relations—without a friend, or companion in this country—surrounded by little girls, whose greatest enjoyment is to tease their schoolmistresses ; foregoing every pleasure, every relaxation, and even necessary wants ; and doing all this *for nothing !* resigning herself to a voluntary torture of two years' pain and monotony, and scarcely getting a kind word in return ! and this, dear, is done heroically, without a murmur or a complaint on her part ! or the *fact of any one ever knowing it.* Isn't it surprising, Nelly? and I look with wonder and admiration on the brave souls who have the fortitude to do this. I hope you are not laughing at me, Nelly, for being so prosy, but I cannot help remarking, from my small experience in these matters, that it is *woman* always that takes advantage of woman's helplessness. It is woman who makes the hard bargain, who is the hard taskmaster, and the still harder paymaster. It is the fault of ladies and schoolmistresses, that governesses are so inhumanly under-paid ! This must not last, or else, really, we shall forfeit all claim to being the *softer* sex.

To come back to our noble Fraulein. She had been slaving without a single reproach escaping her lips for two long years, and had not received one penny value of reward ; and when she had that day received the first acknowledgment of her

dearly-earned services—the miserable payment of her first term
—the joy had been too much for her. The possession of so much
money had turned her wild! but it was not the wildness of any
selfish feeling, she had never intended keeping anything of it
to herself, she had made up her mind to send *every farthing
of it home*, as her first earnings, *to her father and mother*, as
a proof that their absent child still cherished a loving remem-
brance of their parental kindness ; and it was only the prospect
of this happiness, the conviction of the happiness it would be
to her parents when the little parcel fell like a blessing upon
them, that had sent her delirious for the moment, and over-
flooded her simple heart with joy. This the poor German girl
told us in broken English words ; and as our eyes all turned
in shame upon Snapp, the reproach was too much for her, and,
dropping her head, *she slunk out of the room.*

  *   *   *   *·   *

I open this letter a second time to say that we have a grand
concert and ball on Mrs. Rodwell's birth-day, and a supper
(sandwiches and negus) to follow. I must not stay to tell you
about it now, beyond asking you to call on Mamma and beg of
her to send my best evening dress. And mind, Nelly, *you*
come, or you never—never—never will be forgiven by
Your dearest friend
KITTY CLOVER.

Do you think you could bring Sydney as *your married
brother ?* He could lower his hair down on both sides to hide
his want of whiskers.

I forgot to tell you *I am married again ;* only this time I
have taken precious good care to *be the husband.* My wifey is
a pretty, good-tempered, insipidity ; believes everything, works
well at her needle, and has a foot and hand the same size as
mine. We are exceedingly happy, and now I have discovered
the bright side of marriage, I never wish to be divorced again.

P.S. (MOST IMPORTANT). The following rule has just this

moment been stuck up in the study, sentencing " Any young
lady, using improper adjectives, ejaculations, or vulgar exple-
tives, to *pay a fine of five forfeits* for each such inelegant
expression." This is to check what Snapp calls " ladies' pro-
fane language ; " or " female swearing ; " and so we are to be
denied the indulgence of an occasional " *Bother !* " or the
luxury of relieving our feelings every now and then with an
explosive " *Drat it !* " excepting by paying the above
outrageous tax. I should like to know where they think
we are to get all our money from? I am sure our parents
do not give us pocket-money sufficient to encourage these
extravagances ; but I will tell you all about this system of
fines in my next.

THE TWELFTH LETTER LEFT.

(Dated June the 2nd.)

SHOWING VERY PLAINLY WHAT A TAX FORFEITS ARE, AND HOW
   THEY ARE LEVIED;   BESIDES SHOWING HOW YOUNG
   LADIES ARE TAUGHT THE PROPRIETY OF HAVING A GOOD
   CARRIAGE.

ON my word, these forfeits are no joke ! They are not
merely bad marks, or long lessons, or so many hundred
lines to be copied out, or learnt by heart ; but they are actual
fines in hard, *very hard*, money. *Each forfeit is a half-penny
a-piece.* You will say, Nelly, that that is little enough ; but
when they fall down upon you five, or six, or as many as twelve
strong at a time, I can tell you that the blow is rather a heavy
one for a delicate purse. Mine has received so many blows of
the kind that it is perfectly exhausted. Every penny has been
fairly knocked out of it. All my pocket-money has been consumed—all my cakes swallowed—all my sweetmeats melted
one by one, by this devouring system of forfeits ; and I believe

they would gobble up my clothes, bonnets, boots, everything I have, if they only had a chance.

The system, I mean to say, Nelly, is altogether a bad one. To begin, all punishments that are payable by money are bad —at least so I have heard papa say when he has been reading the police reports.   Then, it teaches us *to run into debt*, for if a girl has no more money, she is obliged to borrow some, as no one is allowed to go home until *all her forfeits are paid*. What her debts to her schoolfellows may be is quite another thing !   Then, again, I maintain it is a cruel robbery, almost worse than an income tax, upon us poor girls, for our parents surely never intended when they gave us our pocket-money, that it should find its way, every penny of it, into the school-mistress's pocket ; and, lastly, it makes us suspect all manner of wicked things of our Lady Principal, as we imagine that the money forfeited all goes to her private use, and the girls really believe that one half of her beautiful drawing-room has been furnished in this way.   Whenever a new bonnet comes home, it is curious to hear the buzz of insinuations that instantly, like a swarm of gnats, go flying round the school.   Every girl believes in her heart that she has been taxed for the payment of that bonnet. A system, Nelly, which reduces a schoolmistress in the estimation of her pupils, to the level of very *little better than a thief*, cannot be a very good one !

What makes these suppositions still stronger, is, that the forfeits are levied for the smallest possible fault. If one of your books is lying about ; if your hands are slightly dirty ; if your dress is a little untidy : if you yawn, or gape, or smile, or are guilty of any violation of the five-hundred rules that are stuck up in the school-room, the forfeits immediately rain down upon you in a heavy shower, and there is no place of shelter that can save you.   I have been bankrupt two or three times, and am deeply in debt now, so when you come to see me, Nelly, mind you bring plenty of money (*ten shillings at least*) to help me out of my scrape, and I'll owe it you.

Then, to increase our distress, there are "charities" also,
but I am afraid to touch upon this serious subject, lest you
should shake your pretty head, and decláre that since I have
been at school, I have *grown positively hard-hearted.* No,
dearest Nelly, I hope I am as charitable as most girls. I
know I feel always ready to cry over any case of distress, and
long with all my heart to relieve it. I give what little I can
to the poor, and am pained when I refuse a beggar, for fear he
should *not* be the impostor I have condemned him in my own
mind to be ; but I do not understand the kind of "charity"
that is practised here. We have such numbers of "Distressed
Widows" and "Destitute Orphans," that we cannot help
doubting the reality of a few of them. Scarcely a week passes
without our having a "Broken Leg," or the school being
cleaned out with a "Disastrous Fire." Now, if we *only could
see* a "Widow," and *give her the money ourselves,* or take two
or three of the "Orphans" by the hand, and kiss the little
dears, I am sure we should feel much greater sympathy with
the cases in question, and should be charitable from real
feeling, instead of being as we are now, charitable only from
compulsion. We are always relieving, but never see any of the
objects we relieve, not even a "Broken Leg;" and so the
impression has become rooted in all the girls' minds that these
are all imaginary cases, got up expressly to *teach us* charity, in
the same way that unknown quantities are taken in equations,
to teach us algebra. Now if a real "Widow" was to come in
some day, and thank us in person for what we had done for her,
what a difference it would make ! what is now a task would
be instantly converted into a *pleasure!*

But I must tell you about CAPTAIN MARCH. He is our drilling master. He is not a real captain, you know, but is only
called so out of compliment. (Noble protests he's only a
sergeant, but then that's just like Noble, she'd make out Count
D'Orsay to have been no better than a barber's apprentice.)
He has a beautiful black moustache, and is more than six feet

high, but as stiff as a back-board. His chest perhaps is a little
too large. It looks too much like a carpet-bag when it's *as
full as it can hold*—and Meggy Sharpe doesn't scruple to say
it is exactly in that predicament—but then she is such a *satirical thing !* His coat is scarlet, and it fits, dear, as *tight as a
pincushion.* Of course he is married, or else he wouldn't be
admitted into the college. His wife, they say, is only three
feet high.

We have to wear a peculiar costume for drilling, not unlike
a Bloomer's. It is a short brown-holland blouse, with a red
belt. Our trousers are of the same material, but rather short,
displaying our feet and ankles. We look so funny in it, and
you would laugh to see us. We are placed in rows, and made
to go through all imaginary steps and exercises, like so many
militiamen. We should make a famous regiment, I can tell
you, Nelly, and if the French should ever invade us, we are
ready to turn out to a man—I mean a woman—and defend our
good little Queen, and all her colonies and dominions.

Captain March has a voice like a cannon. I'm sure it must
be heard sometimes at Hyde Park Corner. He makes the
window-panes rattle as he bawls out, " Up—up with your
heads, young ladies. Throw your chests well out—more—more,
I say—in with the waist—bu-u-ulge your chests, ladies ! " And
he swells his own out to that extent, that you imagine it would
burst all the buttons !

Then we have to march quick and slow, the captain walking
by our side, marking the time with a small bamboo-cane,
and crying out, " Right, left—right, left—keep time, pray
keep time, young ladies," (and then he shrieks out, as if he was
going mad) " Where ARE your chests, ladies ? Yes ; that's
better, now. Right, left—mark the cadence properly—right,
left," and so on for an entire hour.

It is glorious fun, Nelly ; only I don't like the captain to
pull me about. It *tickles me so* that I cannot help laughing,
and the consequence is I get fined. There are more forfeits

during our drilling-lesson than any other class.   The captain
pretends to be very angry, but I fancy at times I see him
smiling behind his thick moustache.   With all his black looks,
he is very good-natured, and often persuades Blight (who
remains in the room all the while) to remit us one-half our fines.

But I must haste with my letter, dear, or else MADAME
DUHAUTON will be here directly.   She is our " *Maîtresse de
Maintien*," and has on her cards, " *Brevetée de toutes les
Cours de l'Europe*."   She is as thin as continental-letter-
paper, but excessively elegant, with a waist scarcely larger
than a wedding-ring.   Few mistresses in our school are
respected so much, or followed with so much attention as
Madame Palmyre Duhauton.   Her lessons are most amusing,
instructing us how to balance the body, walk, curtsey, sit,
lounge, meet a friend, enter a carriage, mount on horseback,
get over a style, and be presented at court ! ! !   Her attitudes
alone are a perfect study of deportment.   She sits as if an
artist was in the room ; she walks as though she were
performing before an audience.   Every movement is studied.
She hands you the poker like a Tragedy Queen, and if she
brings you a cup of tea, it is done with the air of an injured
rival offering you a goblet of poison.   But, in spite of all these
affectations, there is an *abandon* (it's her own word), an
elegant freedom about her that wins your admiration at once.
I believe if she were to meet a mad bull she would do it so
gracefully that the animal would immediately draw in his
horns, and politely run away in another direction.

As for " the high walks of Society," which she is always
boasting of having moved in, none of us believe them any more
than that she is a Frenchwoman.   The rumour is, that she is
the widow of an English officer who lived for a long time on
the Continent.   Meggy Sharpe insists that her real name is
D. (Diana) Haughton, which, with the aid of a little French
polish, she has brightened gradually up into De Horton, De
Hauton, Duhauton.

I will try to give you a notion of one of her lessons.

She enters the room with a swimming undulating movement, murmurs softly a "*Bon jour, mes enfants*," and begins at once : " Now, my dear girls, your whole fate hangs upon paying attention.   How often am I to repeat you are to move *vos hanches*—your haunches—and *non vos genoux*—I mean your kneeses ? Mademoiselle Plodder—*écoutez-moi*,—was your papa a *canard ?* or a Greenwich pensioner with two wooden legs ? that you will *boíter* and waddle in that impossible frightful *manière.   Maintenant suivez-moi*, walk like me," and Madame crosses the room backwards and forwards, in the most wavy, dance-like style, to show us how a lady should walk.   " *Là !* *Faites comme ça*, and you will have no reason to *rougir*, not even amongst *la crème de la crème*, at the very top of society. *O ciel !* dear me ! Miss Flower—*arrêtez*—what a meeting ! Did you wish to offer the Monsieur your foot, or your hand ? Great heavens, ladies ! what do you do with your heads ? The gentlemen do not run *comme des lapins* or like cats and dogs upon the floor.   *Allons*, my dear children, *les épaules en arrière—la tête bien haute—bien haute.*   A young lady will never get a husband, now-a-days, unless she holds her head up. *Les marriages*, you know, are written in heaven, and so you must look up *there*, and not on the carpet—*il n'y a pas de maris à present sur le tapis.*"   (Here Madame indulged in a hearty laugh over her own wit—nothing boisterous— but a fashionable titter that wouldn't wake a baby.)   "Ah ! *ça— c'est beaucoup mieux.*   Now, in one minute, it will commence to rain very hard, and you will have to run, for not one of you, mind, has got a *parapluie*, or a parasol.   There ! *je vous l'avais bien dit.*   Run, my dears, run—*vite, plus vite*—but stop, Miss Clover " (and she caught hold of me) ; " you must not pull up your dress so high, *comme si vous alliez prendre un bain de pieds.*"

We hurried through the shower again, and Madame was pleased to say that I ran that time, " *à merveille.*"   We then

G

went through our sitting lesson, and you would have been amused, dear, at the numberless directions that were given how we were to sit on a chair, on a sofa, on a music-stool, at the head of the table, in an open carriage, at the opera, and a thousand other places. I always thought there was only one way of sitting; but I never was more mistaken in all my life. Curtseys followed. "*Merci*, Miss Noble, *merci*," (exclaimed our little French-Englishwoman,) "that curtsey was perfection. It would have been an honour to the Court *du Grand Monarque*. It was *digne d'une Reine*. *Continuez comme ça, ma chère*, and your success is certain. *Je vous prédis un* settlement in the highest ranks. Mademoiselle Wylde!" (she continued) "what do you go for up and down in that way? that is *churning*—not curtseying. *Doucement*, my dear, I do not ask you to make butter;" and she made us all laugh by imitating Lucy's quick movements.

The carriage (an old sofa put upon wheels) was next driven into the middle of the room, and we were taught how to step into it in the most elegant manner. *I* made a sad mess of it, Nelly; and Madame Palmyre was so angry that she went so far as to declare that "no man of taste or pretensions would ever think of uniting his destinies to one so shamefully uneducated in the first steps—(did she mean the carriage-steps?)—of High Life." After this harangue, in which the French accent had been accidentally omitted, I was dismissed in disgrace.

The crowning part of the lesson was the presentation at Court. Madame seated herself on a raised ottoman, which did duty for a throne. The girls retired to a little closet in the corner, from which they emerged in their full Court costume. This consisted of an old window-curtain for the train, and a beautiful group of cut silver-paper feathers for the plumes; and I thought to myself what a capital dress it will make when we play at "*acting charades.*"

"*Bien gracieusement et modestement rendu*, Miss Peacock,"

exclaimed Madame, in a half-majestic tone, from her royal ottoman. "*Ma charmante jeune* Miss, *votre beauté d'une ange et votre tournure d'une Duchesse seront un de ces jours bien appreciées.* Ah! Miss SMIFFEL!—(and here her Majesty rose in the greatest indignation)—Are you mad, or only foolish? Never dare to kiss my hand again until after you have wiped your mouth. I don't know what you have been eating, but it looks uncommonly like gooseberry jam!!!" (True enough, there was a large jar, belonging to the Suetts, in the closet, and Smiffel had helped herself rather liberally— robing and robbing at the same time.) "Learn, ladies, that only a very slight pressure of the lips is permitted. Now, Ada Steele, what are you afraid of? Her Majesty is not going to slap your face that you should look so alarmed to kiss her hand. Well, Miss St. Ledger, am I to repeat again and again that I will not have you come rolling up to the steps of my throne like a cricket-ball? Pray learn to moderate your bounding enthusiasm. But good heavens! girl, your *feather has touched my face.* Ill-bred creature! Would you presume to *tickle her Majesty's nose with your Court Plume?* But I absolve myself from all responsibility of your future destinies. With such innate vulgarity, it's preposterous to suppose you ever can or WILL BE MARRIED!!"

With this extraordinary speech from the throne, Madame descended the footstools which had been arranged as a flight of steps. What struck me most during the delivery was, the perfect Queen's English—for *une native de Paris,* especially— in which it was spoken; but, as it was the Queen, and not Madame in her own person, who was speaking, it may, perhaps, account for the extraordinary phenomenon and the fidelity of the representation. Nature only sacrificed herself to truth. However, with the loss of her foreign royalty, she soon recovered the use of her native tongue, and, smiling a Frenchwoman's smile, she said to Noble, "*Ayez la bonté, ma chère, de prendre ma place.*" She then showed us how the Queen was to be respectfully approached, how her hand was to be gently kissed, and how the *débutante* was to carefully withdraw, without being incommoded with, or falling over her train. With this last performance, which, I must say, Nelly, was admirably done, the Levee was at an end.

I had nearly forgotten to tell you that, during the above ceremony, Noble and Peacock wore their own feathers and their own trains. Their pride couldn't think of being dragged about the floor in connection with *an old window-curtain!*

Good-bye, Nelly; and don't forget to bring the money, if you wish to save from bankruptcy and shame,

Your devoted, but penniless, friend,

KITTY.

P.S. Last night was the *first Friday in the month, and a full moon!* so we resolved upon trying our luck when we went to bed. Accordingly, we made all haste in undressing, and put the candles out very quickly. We then placed ourselves in a row, with the *moonbeams full in our faces;* after which, upon a given signal from Wylde, we repeated slowly the following words:—

> "Upon this month's lucky Friday,
> Beneath the moonbeam's magic ray,
> Stepping backwards into my bed,
> I pray, benevolent St. John,·
> To show in nightly vision,
> The husband I on earth shall wed."

These were delivered as solemnly as possible: as soon as they were over, without uttering another sound, we walked backwards into bed, keeping our faces turned all the time to the moon, and so dropped off to sleep.

If any one speaks, they say the charm is broken. It is confidently reported (Susan told us so, and she had it from a gipsey) that *it is sure to succeed* if repeated precisely as the clock strikes twelve, finishing the last word with the last stroke ; but we were afraid of oversleeping ourselves, or that some of the younger girls might grow frightened, or that the moonbeams might not shine, so we wisely preferred saying it beforehand. If you *tell* your dream, you will never be married ; but as I never dreamt of any one (not even of Sydney, much to my disappointment), there is no great fear of my dying an old maid on that score at least. It is a thousand pities, Nelly, that the chances are so many against the above charm succeeding. It has often been tried here, but some girl has always spoken, or shrieked by falling against something and hurting herself in walking backwards. The greatest difficulty, however, is in *preventing the girls talking ;* but we two will try it some night, Nell, only we must promise *not to tell each other our dreams !* The penalty would be too awful ! !

THE THIRTEENTH LETTER LEFT.

(Dated June 9.)

SHOWING HOW FOOLISH IT IS TO PLAY PRACTICAL JOKES.

THAT Lizzy Spree is as full of tricks as a Pantomime ! She is quite a spoilt child in the way of mischief. She has been allowed so many indulgences that she imagines she may empty powder-boxes into bonnets, and place detonating-balls under chairs, just as she pleases. She's *a sad torment.* It's not safe to leave the snuffers even with her. She's sure to fill them with scraped slate-pencil, or else gunpowder. It's my belief she always carries a stock of the latter in her pocket, so as never to lose an opportunity of making us all jump out of our skins. It's like a constant succession of postmen's knocks

to be with her, you are leaping up every minute until you hardly
know whether your heart is in your mouth or not.   Her last
trick was to fill Professor Drudge's snuff-box with Cayenne
pepper.   I'm sure the old gentleman sneezed to that extent
that we had to stuff our pocket-handkerchiefs into our mouths,
to *prevent ourselves dying of laughing* ; but that wasn't so bad
as her rubbing a lot of cobbler's wax inside old Miss Penelope's
chapeau de dimanche, so that when she pulled it off, cap and
wig came off with it, and exposed to view the *funniest little
bald head* you ever saw !

However her love of mischief has brought her into trouble.
I don't suppose Lizzy, with her kind heart, would intentionally
hurt any one, but she has been terribly punished for her habit
(and I think it's a very silly habit) of practical joking.

We were all in the garden, trying to knock down with our
skipping ropes the little hard unripe pears, when up runs Spree
to Owen, quite out of breath, and begins screaming—" Mary,
Mary, dear, there's such a fine, military gentleman, asking for
you in the parlour.   Make haste !   *It is your Father ! ! !* "

Scarcely were the words uttered, than off darted Owen with
all her speed, looking so wild, and followed by Darling, and
a whole string of girls—Spree amongst us vainly trying
to call us back.   I got to the parlour-door, only just in time to
see Owen fall senseless into the arms of—what a wicked, wicked
shame !—of Strong, *the shoemaker !* who had come to measure
us for our winter boots.

You cannot imagine the painful scene that followed.   There
was Darling, screaming over poor Mary, who was lying apparently lifeless on the floor.   There was Blight rubbing her
temples and hands with *Eau de Cologne*.   There was Spree
crying, the Lady Principal scolding ; and the whole College
mounted on tables and chairs, crowding round, all of us moved
to tears by the agonising result before us of the cruel joke.   We
all thought she was killed.   No one (except Mrs. Rodwell) had
the courage to reproach Spree.   Her own suffering was suffi-

cient punishment. She accused herself of being the cause of Mary's death ; of having murdered her by her unfeeling levity; and went and knelt down by the side of the poor sufferer, begging, crying piteously, for forgiveness.

Mary, at last, began to revive. She slowly opened her eyes ; but, oh, Nelly ! there was such intense despair in the wild, enquiring look she cast round the room ! there was such anguish in the groan that escaped from her white lips, that I almost regretted she had ever recovered to return to her life of suffering again !

For many days, Mary Owen seemed unconscious, as if the heavy blow had stunned mind and feeling. She permitted Amy's caresses ; and at times would play with Lizzy's hair, and wipe her tears away, when the unhappy girl came to her bedside, and began reproaching herself for having laid her there. She got better after a time ; but when she came down, it was like one walking in her sleep. We all moved away for fear of waking her. Her spirit seemed gone, as if it had been startled away from her gentle bosom (for she never did harm to any body), when the only hope that nestled there had been so cruelly made to fly away. We all felt that she could not long remain with us. I imagined that the finger of Death had already touched those vacant eyes, and left its chill upon those bloodless lips. The school grew silent. It couldn't have been quieter in holiday-time. Our only amusement seemed to be in paying attention to poor Mary, and hers was the greatest pleasure who succeeded in paying her the most. The Lady Principal, even, generally so stern, was touched by her uncomplaining agony. She grew kind and considerate, grasping hold of every little opportunity to soothe her with a mother's care. Dr. Healy shook his head. " The case," he said, " was beyond the skill of medicine." This opinion fell like a frost upon our hopes, and we watched with a sympathy that grew greater every day, the silent grief that was consuming a fond heart, that really seemed dying for the want of an object to love.

One Sunday afternoon, the seniors were allowed to sit in the little drawing-room with Owen. She was lying on the sofa, wrapt round with shawls, more dreaming than awake, exhausted by long pain, and perfectly insensible to our efforts to amuse her.   Amy had just been reading to her some poetry, in a voice that seemed to speak from Heaven—so sweet and pure was it, Nelly,—when Mrs. Rodwell entered looking pale and excited. She drew a seat near Mary, and, taking her hand, began in a softened voice to speak about the comforts of religion.   We all bent our heads, and listened.   She said, dear, more beautiful things than I can ever think of repeating, and said them so impressively, that my heart felt being gradually drawn towards hers, and as if it would melt into tears.   We scarcely knew the object of this exhortation—but a cold horror crept over us —could *Mary be dying?*   Had the Lady Principal come to prepare her for death ?—to comfort her last thoughts ?—and to atone with a few last moments of kindness for the little that Mary had ever received from her hands ? But the words of truth, as they came forth like light, dispelled all these dark suspicions. Little by little—and gradually—like a stubborn heart's repen-tance—the sense changed its sadness ; it broke like a beautiful dawn into peace—peace brightened with a thousand rays into hope ; and hope filled us with a celestial joy that made us love all things.   I was no longer a school-girl, Nelly, full of pride, and folly, and vanity ; but something much better.   I felt *strong enough for anything*, and longed to go forth and do good, and comfort poor creatures, as our good schoolmistress was then intent upon doing ; and I inwardly resolved I would no longer think harshly of her, or of any one, as my soul accused me of having too often done !

We listened and listened, purified and strengthened with the supporting words, and, after a while, the cheering tones of happiness stole, like the beautiful summer air, over poor Owen's drooping spirit, and instilled fresh life into it.   A look of gratitude shone from her loving eyes upon the speaker, and showed how sensible she yet was to kindness; but beyond this all efforts to revive her failed. No tenderness would heal the mortally-wounded heart! The love had come too late—the nourishment had arrived when there was nothing to nourish!

Mrs. Rodwell ceased speaking. She saw the power of listening had gone. Rising softly, she beckoned Amy out of the room, and they left noiselessly together. After a few moments' absence, Amy returned, her face flushed, and full of burning secrets. Quietly motioning us away, she fell on her knees by the side of the sofa, and, in a voice that flowed with tears, began telling Owen one of the simple little tales that used to be her favourite enjoyment to listen to. It was all about foreign lands—about a wanderer far from home—separated from his only child—longing to embrace his darling daughter, —but still kept in exile by the cruel necessity of a soldier's life. At last the anxious father sends a bosom friend as a messenger of joy to his darling one; and then Amy, trembling with emotion, twining her arms as in a love-wreath round Owen's neck, and frightened to death—of which her face was the living picture — about the result of her intelligence, and, cautiously as a mother moves her sleeping infant, told Owen that news had arrived from her father " *that he lived*, and had sent a friend freighted with the treasures of his love, who was waiting outside to deliver his trust."

At first we thought Mary had not understood, and Amy repeated more positively the fact. Then silently caressing her friend's agitated face, Owen sorrowfully shook her head, incapable of belief; but upon Amy's insisting upon the truth, and assuring her repeatedly (and each assurance was sealed with a kiss) that " she would not deceive her for the world," tears slowly overflowed her pale cheeks, and she sighed sorrowfully; but not a word escaped her lips. Amy at last, almost despairing to revive hopes, that had once been so heartlessly cheated, asked Owen " if she thought she felt strong enough to see her father's friend?" There was no reply to this question—not the slightest sign of intelligence — but a fixed statue-like expression came over the bewildered girl, and she remained immoveable like the reclining figures I have seen on the tombs in cathedrals ; all other efforts failed to re-animate her.

When she had closed her eyes, Amy left the room. She returned the next moment, leading by the hand a middle-aged gentleman, with beautiful silver-white hair. Upon his entrance, Owen seemed convulsed. She fixed her eyes so upon him that I grew frightened. She then rubbed them as though to satisfy herself whether she was dreaming—and stared again, as if she couldn't believe her eyesight. She then pressed her hands upon her forehead—her mouth opened widely—her whole frame heaved and trembled with excess of feeling ; and, rising slowly from her couch, she would have fallen to the ground, if her *father* had not been happily by her side to receive her in his arms.

And there we left them, Nelly, the pale, corpse-like head resting peacefully on the bosom so long and hopelessly desired !

They have been together ever since. Mary was dangerously ill, but her father's tenderness and the hand of Mercy have lifted her off a bed of sickness. Each day, happiness (that joyful artist to whom so few of us sit for our portraits) colours her cheeks with an additional touch of beauty, her eyes begin to sparkle and to speak—and her lips surprise themselves sometimes with a smile, and, I have no doubt, when sufficiently tutored, will be advanced into the higher class of laughter. And this has all been done under the tuition of Love, the best mistress after all, Nelly, when we wish to improve by learning *things by heart.* So rapid, too, is Mary's progress under his scholarship, that I shouldn't wonder if she is the prettiest girl in the school yet.

Colonel Owen never leaves his daughter's side. He seems never to tire of patting and fondling his darling, or of rejoicing with Amy, or thanking the Lady Principal in terms of unbounded gratitude " for her motherly care and tenderness to his lonely child." Poor father! *if he only knew all*—but he never will be told of his daughter's many years of suffering. The reward of injury is the luxury of forgiveness, and Mary, who has well earned the reward, seems to revel in the luxury as a thing too sweet to be parted with. Besides, I doubt if all recollection of former slights has not been completely rubbed out, like a sum on a slate, of her forgiving mind. The affectionate tending of the last few days is alone remembered. She is too gratefully happy for even a *memory of sorrow*. Her heart, dear, is so replete with love, it can exclude none from its embrace, not even its enemies.

As for Amy, she and Mary are like too sisters (without the jealousy). She has told her father of her beloved friend's untiring life of kindness to her and to all who are in want of it. The Colonel loves her almost like a second daughter, and makes her presents till she doesn't know how to accept them, or how to refuse them. The last one was a gold heart, with the name of "Mary" engraved on it, and inside a bit of Mary's hair, that was cut off in the fever during which Amy nursed her night and day. They are to pass the holidays together.

Oh! I nearly forgot to tell you that they went to the Opera on Tuesday night, and took Lizzy Spree with them. The foolish girl made her eyes quite red with crying. The Colonel knows nothing about the cause of Mary's illness.

There, Nelly ; the above subject has so engrossed all my thoughts and paper, that I have only just spare time left— (class bell's ringing)—to sign myself

Your dearest, dearest friend,

KITTY.

THE FOURTEENTH LETTER LEFT.

(The smallest possible size of a Lady's note.)

SHOWING HOW A YOUNG LADY CAN LEAVE OUT THE MOST
IMPORTANT PART OF HER LETTER.

DEAREST NELLY,—I was nearly leaving out the Post-
script of my last letter. How extremely foolish! I
now send it to you.

Poor little Twigg is in disgrace. The pianoforte-tuner has
made her an offer of marriage, and the Lady Principal not only
won't let her accept it, but says *she ought to be ashamed of
herself*—indulging in such good-for-nothing fancies, and setting
such a bad example to the young ladies of the establishment.
Twigg carries his portrait in her huswife, amongst all the
pins and needles. I cannot say whether he is good-looking,
because she has cried over it to that extent that the colour
has been completely washed all over his face, and purple
eyes and blue whiskers do not exactly give him the most pre-
possessing appearance. She says her heart is broken, and, as
far as one can judge, she eats nothing. She seems to live only
upon tears. She declares her hopes are blighted, and doesn't
mind how soon she dies. We pity Twigg; and many are the
consolations which are given her by girls who say they have
suffered as great, if not greater hardships—and how they
ever *survived it* was a miracle! but, considering how fat
some of them look now, their grief seems to have agreed
with them remarkably well. In fact, Miss Isabella's crying
has given quite a tone of sentiment to the school, and some
of the sighs you hear would turn a windmill. The struggle with
each girl seems to recollect the period when she was most

miserable, and if she can only prove that she has known more misery than anyone else, then she is supremely happy. I cannot tell you how tired I am of this wishy-washy stuff. I have no patience with martyrs of fourteen, who wish to go into a convent, and pray for the tomb to open and receive them; when, if an invitation to a ball came, they would be clapping their hands with joy, and soon be lost in a long debate as to what dress they should wear. I declare there have fallen so many showers of tears lately that the school feels quite damp. Fraulein is the worst. She would be invaluable to a gardener; for I am sure she cannot weep less than a watering-potfull at a time. Her sentiment, too, makes you so melancholy that I am sure it is not safe to leave so many bodkins about. I wish to gracious! the Lady Principal would let Twigg marry, for all the girls have so completely made her injuries their own, that it is nothing but a flutter of pocket-handkerchiefs all day long. What can they know of suffering, Nelly, in comparison with ME? and I am sure one look from Sydney, when he goes by on the top of an omnibus, is worth all their pianoforte-tuners in the world!

If Twigg wasn't such a favourite, there wouldn't be so much fuss made about her. She is the junior governess, and some day is to inherit Mrs. Rodwell's black velvet mantle. She has never been away from the Princess' College, and doesn't know what holidays are. The whole world is only a big school to her! The consequence is, she is *a great overgrown bread-and-butter school-girl*, though she's thirty-two years old, if she's a day. They say she was pretty once; but for the life of me I cannot see her beauty. She is so conceited—so stuck-up, prim, and affected, always showing off to the masters, and flirting with Herr Hullabullützer. She is so much in love with herself, that I wonder she ever found any to spare for the poor piano-forte tuner (who by the way, has been ordered never to come into the house again). We do just what we like with Twigg, by flattering her. Even the little girls coax her over by telling her what pretty hair she has, or asking to feel the softness of her hand. By these means they get excused many a forfeit, and let off many a hard task.

No wonder she has got such a soft hand, or that it is so white, when the story goes that *she sleeps in gloves*, and that she is always washing it with *pâte d'amandes*. No wonder either that her ringlets are so glossy, when she spends one half her income in cosmetics and Circassian creams ; and is twisting and. twirling them round her fingers all the time she is not eating !

It's a world of pity she is so weak, for really, Nelly, she is very good-natured—and clever in her little way—and quite grateful if we only admire her. I think we are often tempted to praise her more than we otherwise should, on account of the great pleasure it gives her. If we only ask to dress her hair, she is as pleased as if she was going to the play. Besides I don't know what we should do without Twigg, for she buys our goodies, gets whatever we want in town, and posts our letters (many a one has she posted for you, Nelly !) On the other hand, we tell her all manner of stories about our brothers, how they admired her at the last concert ; and invent love messages from our cousins. They are every one of them *stricken* with her. She takes in every word, and goes to sleep with her head as full of dreams as of curl-papers. If anything very particular is wanted—a supper, for instance, on a large scale—Twigg will procure us the pork pies, the peppermint, tarts, and all, if we only promise to write home about her, and invite her in the holidays. In this way, I believe, the poor girl has got ten invitations for next holidays—and, in her simple soul, believes she will go to every one of them. Her conceit plays all sorts of tricks with her. She is continually fancying gentlemen are looking at her, and falling in love at first sight. She carries a locket with a hair chain in her bosom. Whenever her aunt scolds her, she takes out this locket, and begins crying. By this we suspect that it is the *souvenir* of some early disappointment—long before the piano-forte tuner—perhaps the dancing-master? But with all her curious old school-girlish ways, we cannot help pitying Twigg. Her greatest fault is her vanity. It is the sun round which her nature revolves. Place her in the desert with a looking-glass, and she would be as happy as a woman in a bonnet-shop.

I must now run away to our singing-mistress, SIGNORA PRECIOSA-NINI—a real Neapolitan, though it puzzles me to understand how " *crater* " can be the Italian pronunciation of " creature." She teaches us *effect*, and she was to have come out at San Carlo, only she lost her stage voice at the very time that Rossini had prophesied she would be the first Prima Donna in the world. *It was grief that did it!* On my word, the world seems to be full of nothing but grief; only it's rather profitable to the Signora. She works it into all her songs, and sells them at the rate of two shillings a copy. Such miserable subjects, Nelly; everyone is disappointed, or driven to despair, or dying in them. I think if the world grew virtuous, and there were no more hearts broken, the music-sellers would have to shut-up shop.

There was such a knocking at the door last night. It lasted for at least a quarter of an hour. The belief is that it was Mrs. Rodwell's husband come back *to ask for some more money.* The wretch!

THE FIFTEENTH LETTER LEFT.

(*Dated June 15th.*)

SHOWING HOW A LONG PURSE IS SOMETIMES NEEDED AT SCHOOL
TO MAKE IT "THE HAPPIEST TIME OF OUR LIVES."

I SHOULD have written before, dearest Eleanor, if I had not been reduced to poverty. I have actually been incapable of paying Susan's postage fee. There is not a Queen's-head even left in my purse. Almost everything has been cleared out of the pretty workbox that dear Fanny Jackson gave me before she went away to the North, and I have scarcely anything left to raise a loan with. But, worse than all, I am 2s. 4½d. in debt!

It was cruel of you, Nelly, not to have sent me some money. I wouldn't have asked you, dear, unless I really wanted it; for what with forfeits, mistresses' birthdays, charity, and our system of "mothers," it is nothing but pay, pay, pay, all day long.

You mustn't start, Nell, if I tell you that I am a "mother," and I can assure you I find it anything but agreeable. All the elder girls are supposed to be "mothers;" that is to say, two or three tiresome little plagues are placed under their care, and they are responsible for their clean faces, tidy clothes, and good behaviour. This system is established, as Miss Priscilla observes, in order that "the heart and affections may be culti-vated with the mind, and woman fitted for the sphere of love she is born to adorn." It rather *unfits* me than otherwise, for I can assure you it is as much as I can do to attend to myself, without having a family to look after. When I was *married to Sharpe*, I had her children to nurse, and wash, and scrub as well, so that I was the "mother" of four children, and I am afraid to tell you what a deal of anxiety they cost me,—to say nothing of the forfeits I was continually paying for them. I find education is a very expensive thing, Nelly, and my *worries* have certainly had one good effect; they have taught me *to be more grateful for the education I am myself receiving.*

Sharpe's children were much more unruly than my own. They were always in trouble, and do what I would, I couldn't keep their hands clean. I was constantly getting fined, because they would leave their books about the house, or because their hair was rough, or because the little things would persist in biting their nails. I half suspect Miss Meggy Sharpe taught them many faults, in order that I might get punished for the correction of them. At the time I was trying all I could to get a divorce from her, I know she left nothing undone *to spite me*, and it is my firm belief it was she who directed them to steal the thin bread and butter, the more especially *as she ate it all herself.* I was taking my music lesson at the time, and the little plagues were planted on the staircase, where they waylaid Susan as she was carrying the tea-tray up to the drawing-room, and emptied all the plates. This they did not once, but actually twice. Susan was scolded, she cried, and told the truth. The young things were sent for, and I was ready, dear, to drop through the floor when I heard those wicked little Peppercorns tell the Lady Principal, "*It warn't their faults, their mother had made them do it.*" Oh, Nelly, I protested I knew nothing about it, that I wasn't fond of bread and butter ; it was all to no purpose—the impudent young story-tellers were believed in preference to *me*, and I was *fined fifty forfeits,* besides being sentenced to a week's "*silence.*" Of course, when I went into the school-room I had it out instantly with Meggy Sharpe, but she only laughed at me, and my week's punishment was increased to two, for having dared to break through the rules so soon. My troubles were not yet over, for what did the malicious creature do, but she assembled the senior girls round me, and began telling them such *great big stories* about my engagement to Sydney, revealing all I had foolishly confided to her honour, and adding considerably to it. She then completed her cruelty by *reading out aloud to them Sydney's last beautiful letter,* making fun of every sweet expression and turning all its tender vows of love into ridicule. Each word went like a pair of scissors into my heart ; but much as I suffered, I daren't say a word, for if I had given vent to my indignation, the first syllable would have cost me probably an additional week of "*silence.*" Miss Margaret knew this well enough, and gloried in her revenge for my having ever left her. She is cleverer than I am, Nelly, but only turns her cleverness into acts of cruelty. I did not envy the meanness of her triumph, though I cried my eyes out with vexation, until Amy, who is the guardian angel of everybody, not only

H

put a stop to the *fun*, but even got me Sydney's dear letter
back again.   I consoled myself by reading it over several times
to myself.

Yesterday I was let off the remainder of my severe
punishment.   In the same afternoon, Miss Priscilla addressed
us in a neat speech, reminding us that " our esteemed pre-
ceptress' natal day was fast approaching, when she knew our
affectionate hearts would only be too desirous to present
some *trifling* offering as a loving memento of our grateful
respect."   All the school was unanimous in this proposition,
and Noble was appealed to, as head-monitress, for her opinion
about what would be the most acceptable gift.   A workbox, a
desk, an inkstand, a dressing-case was each in its turn
proposed, but all of them rejected, as having been accepted
on previous birthdays.   Then the modest Priscilla came
generously to our aid.   " She knew our beloved instructress
had long desired a timepiece to decorate the mantelpiece of
her *boudoir*, and by a strange coincidence, as felicitous as it
was fortuitous, she had recently expressed much admiration for
one seen in Regent-street ; " but Priscilla kindly feared the
price would exceed our wishes, prodigal as she knew they
were.   Although no one appreciated better than herself the
affectionate attachment which bound the entire College in ties
of motherly love to her sister, still she could not permit any
giddy extravagance, the more especially as Mrs. Rodwell
would value the simplest offering as highly as the richest
gift.   As a friend, therefore, she would request us frankly to
say if we could afford nine guineas :—for such was the price
of the desired clock."   Again was the school unanimous, and
Noble undertook to say, " we could easily manage it."

A small committee was then formed ; Noble was elected to
the honourable post of banker, and Priscilla headed the list
with a donation of half-a-guinea, " begging, however, that it
might not be taken as any intention of what the subscriptions
should be."   I had already emptied my purse on a collection

the week before, and if it had not been for Amy, who lent me
five shillings, I shouldn't have been able to subscribe the
additional sum that was wanted on this occasion. I should like
to have put down a great deal more, to give pleasure to our Lady
Principal, who, after all, has a number of good qualities, and
who has greatly endeared herself to our affections by her
recent kindness to Mary Owen. I have no doubt I should like
her very much, *if she wasn't our schoolmistress*, but somehow
that fact does freeze the fountain of one's love a little bit !

We had hard work to accumulate the nine guineas—for
some girls are more stingy than others ; and it is not always
the richest who are the most liberal. I must say, it pained
me to witness the numerous coaxings, and threats, and petty
artifices that were called into requisition to induce the little
girls to part with their shillings and sixpences ; but what
grieved me most was to see the *begging-box*—(it is a hard
term, Nelly, but really it was very little better)—being carried
round to the poor schoolmistresses, and their being *compelled*
to give—for, if any one of them had refused or complained, it
would have been as much as her situation was worth. In this
way I saw Blight put down half-a-sovereign, which seemed to
be all she had in her purse ; and little Fraulein, too, had to
change one of the golden treasures she had put aside to send
to her parents in order to pay her subscription. Surely, it is
not right to make the small pittance they receive even smaller
by asking them to contribute to these forced compliments.

At last, the necessary sum was scraped together, and a
deputation of happy girls—guarded by Snapp (our *Snap-
Dragon*, as we call her)—started one fine morning, and
brought back the beautiful clock (an ormolu figure of Minerva
seated on the world, teaching a fat little Cupid in bronze his
celestial globe)—and we had, besides, an ice and a bun apiece
at Farrance's. Then begun the mysterious preparations.
Snapp wrote the speech, and little Minnie Campbell, who is
the youngest girl in the school, learnt it, but not until she

had been scolded by Snapp to that degree that when the little thing was taken up before Mrs. Rodwell, in her best Sunday frock, to recite it, she burst into tears, and forgot it all. Snapp had to deliver the speech, with all its long words, herself.

To-morrow is the grand day, and we are in such a flutter that we can talk and think of nothing else. I must leave you, Nelly, as I must run to look after my dress.

I remain, dearest,

Yours, in a perfect fever of excitement,

KITTY CLOVER.

I wish those boys at Dr. Hawkes' would learn to behave themselves! We never meet them but they try to break our ranks, and go on in the most ridiculous manner. They blow kisses to us, and throw up their eyes as if they were dying, and put their hands upon their hearts, and say the most impudent things as we pass. I declare it's quite disagreeable to come near them. Their conduct, too, in church, is so disgraceful that I am astonished the beadle doesn't turn them all out! I do detest boys, Nelly; and these seem to be the rudest, the very worst-behaved specimens I ever saw. What do you think one silly overgrown hobbedehoy, with a turn-down collar and a monkey-jacket, had the impertinence to throw into my parasol as we were out walking last Wednesday? Why, a letter, dear!—and it was *written on a sheet torn out of an exercise-book!* It began with, "Vision of Beauty!— Deign to cast thy cerulean orbs of beauty"—I didn't read any more of the rubbish. How different to dear Sydney's!!!

Talking of that, Nelly, you mustn't say a word about Meggy Sharpe's reading his letter out aloud to the school. It would only make him unhappy, poor fellow; and he would naturally imagine I was in the habit of showing his treasured correspondence to everybody.

P.S. Mind you bring the money with you, Nelly, or else I shall not be allowed to go home ; for no girl is allowed to leave this place in debt. You wouldn't wish me, dearest, to miss my holidays for the matter of a 2s. 4½d., and *I have so much to tell you*, Nelly !

THE SIXTEENTH LETTER LEFT.

(Date blotted out this time, decidedly with tears.)

SHOWING WHAT WAS THE CAUSE OF THE POSTPONEMENT OF THE BALL.

TO-MORROW is our grand ball, Nelly; but all thoughts of the coming joy have been put aside. Our dresses have been brought out in all their smartness ; but they lie upon our beds, untouched, almost unnoticed. There is sorrow, dear, in the house, and every tongue is still as if the grief were its own, and not another person's.

Mrs. Dove is so ill, that when you look at her you are obliged to turn your head for fear of making her grief greater by any exhibition of your own. You long to relieve her—you advance to offer what little aid you can—but tears quickly warn you to retreat, and you feel that the greatest charity is to leave her alone ; that, after all, the best sympathy your heart can show is that of silence. There is such sanctity about her sorrow that you imagine the only words to approach it with should be those of prayer.

Ever since the confirmation she has been growing thinner and paler. She has avoided everybody. She has moved about as if in pain ; and lately has seemed too weak, even, to play with her boy. When you questioned her—"it was only a headache—she could assure you there was nothing the matter —perhaps it was the heat? however she should be better in a

day or two ; " and, do what you would, you could not persuade.
her to have any advice.

Last Sunday she fainted in church, causing a commotion
which brought a letter of complaint from the Rev. Mr. Whyte
Choker the following day.   The Lady Principal was very cross
—and to listen to her reproaches you would imagine that Mrs.
Dove had done it on purpose.   She attributed it entirely to
her " delicacy," and made some harsh remarks about " *ladies*
always taking care to choose the best opportunity for fainting."
But Blight was of a different opinion.   She thought there was
more illness in the accident than purpose or affectation ; and
she redoubled her attentions to her sister-teacher, dressing her
boy of a morning, encouraging her in all her tasks, and helping
her as much as she could.   The first visit, too, Dr. Healy
made, she waylaid him on the staircase, and told him how she
feared the poor young widow was seriously ill.   They went
together to the Lady Principal, and then Mrs. Dove was
summoned to the *boudoir*.   She stood at the door with her
hand upon the handle, for full five minutes, before she dared
go in !

She came out, dear Nelly, supported by Blight, and weeping
violently.   She was holding her boy convulsively to her breast,
as if afraid that some one was about to tear him away from
her ; and, though her kind supporter was offering every consolation her good heart could think of, still it was evident that
not one word entered her ears, or had the slightest effect in
stilling the tempest of her passion.   Her soul was deafened with
the loud noise of its own grief too much to listen, at that
moment, to the gentle voice of kindness.   All entreaties failed,
and, crying as if her heart must break, we saw her carried upstairs to bed, where at least her anguish would be undisturbed
by noise and prying looks.

As soon as Blight came down we gathered round her, and she
told us the Doctor had said it was " a rapid consumption," and
that she would not live a month, unless immediate change of

air and scene were procured.   He strictly forbade her looking
into a book, and solemnly cautioned her, as she loved her child,
and wished to save his life, neither to sleep with him, nor to
caress him—in short, not to allow him to be with her more
than she could positively help.   In fact, to be plain, if she
could make up her mind to a total separation, it would *be better
both for her and for the boy.*

This decision hurt her (so Blight said) a thousand times more
than the knowledge of her own serious illness.   For that she
seemed to care but little, but to be told that she must be separated from the only object that made life sweet, seemed to
stab her to the heart.   To see her boy outstretch his little
arms, and to be obliged to turn away and deny him the kisses
he was begging for, was a privation of affection that her
mother's whole nature revolted at !   Her child was her only
happiness in this world ; and now she musn't indulge in *that !*
nay, worse, she must deny herself all intercourse with him,
and, blinding her eyes to his endearing smiles, she must walk
away with greater indifference even than if the child had been
a stranger's !   It was a dreadful struggle, which Blight hopes
she may never see again.   The baby was crying to go to his
distressed mother, and she was shrinking from him, and
creeping round the table to avoid his childish caresses.   Then
she snatched him up wildly, and covered him with frantic kisses ;
then, as suddenly, she turned aside her head, as though there
were poison in her breath, and she was afraid that one particle
of it might fall upon him, and wither the only flower of her life.
Unclasping his arm from round her neck, she laid him gently
down, and rushed madly to the opposite side of the room, where
she fell exhausted upon the floor.   Whilst she was insensible
her child was carried away.

At this point, Blight, whom we were all thanking for her
sisterly kindness, was called out to assist at a general council.
There were present all the governesses, including Twigg, and
of course the redoubtable Snapp.   Miss Priscilla Hextra was

leaning against the corner of the mantel-piece, and the Lady Principal presided at the head of the rosewood table, wringing her hands as if she was washing them, which is a habit of her's whenever the boiled mutton is too underdone, or she is at all *put out* by any little scholastic excitement. " What was to be done ? She had assumed a very false position in receiving Mrs. Dove with her infant into the school ; and she would take very good care she never did such a foolish thing again ! It was wrong of her to allow feeling to silence judgment ; and now she bitterly repented of it. The facts were these. Mrs. Dove had formerly been educated at her College, and a very good pupil she was. Well, after the death of her profligate husband, she had consented, much out of pity, to accept a small premium— an exceedingly small premium—to maintain them in comfort until a situation could be found for the mother as a governess, which duty she was sorely afraid she would never be qualified to fulfil. However, that trifle had long ago been consumed—in fact, it had barely covered the first year's expenditure. Now, she *was the last person to behave unfeelingly or to wish to turn them out of the house ;* but she wanted to know what was to become of them ? She really could not afford the expense of a lingering illness, that, for anything she knew, might terminate fatally ; and then the child would be left destitute upon her hands. As for property, she knew Mrs. Dove had parted with everything to enable her to enter the College ; and as for relations, both her father and mother were dead, and she doubted if she had a respectable friend in the world. One thing, however, was certain. Mrs. Dove *must appeal for aid elsewhere.* She did not wish to be harsh ; but still the exigencies of the case were such as to render her immediate removal from the Princesses' College a matter of unavoidable necessity. It was preposterous to suppose she could permit a death in her house. It might be fatal to the interests of her establishment. The parents might take alarm—might fancy it was some contagious or infectious disease—and in less than a week all the young ladies might be fetched away, to the great benefit of Mrs. Spankit, who, she had no doubt, would be delighted to receive every one of her pupils. No ; it was a source of great grief for her to say so ; but Mrs. Dove must leave as soon as her health, for which she entertained the greatest anxiety, would permit, and, as for the boy, *he must be removed instantly.*"

Blight pleaded, dearest Nelly, as if she had been pleading for her life. She only asked for *charity for a dying widow.*" She spoke with all the eloquence of a woman's heart ; but there was no woman's heart to listen to her. The Lady Principal had steeled herself in alarm—had regularly encased herself in a full-length suit of selfish fears—and there was no touching her in any one point. She was impenetrable to pity, and to all the noble feelings which generally touch a woman's nature, and make her hold out the hand of charity to another in distress. The governesses promised to subscribe amongst themselves for any additional expense she might be put to on account of the illness of Mrs. Dove ; but no, the *respectability* of the establishment must be considered above all things—and she felt herself bound to refuse their offer, though she was profoundly moved by the generosity of it. The battle was over. Poor Blight abandoned the attack in hopeless discomfiture, finding that her appeals to kindness only flew off blunted and pointless from the hard armour of calculation in which her mistress had arrayed herself for the occasion.

(Oh, I thought to myself all the time I was listening to these sorrowful particulars, if this cruelty had only been known before the subscriptions were collected for the Lady Principal's birthday-present, every girl would have flung all her money out of the window sooner than have subscribed a single shilling for *that* beautiful time-piece !)

Well, Nelly, after a long hour had been spent in useless talk and tears, the council was breaking up, when the Lady Principal, alarmed probably by a cry of her awakening conscience, called them back, and made this concession :

" Poor Mrs. Dove might linger through her few remaining
days in peace at the College, provided the boy were immediately removed to some more appropriate abode, and a
guarantee given for the expenses of the funeral." Blight
instantly gave her own word as a guarantee for the latter
(how can she do it, Nelly, with all her recent claims ? but it's
my firm belief that the girls won't *allow her to pay a farthing
of them,* supposing it ever should come to a struggle of emula-
tion, which I *pray with all my heart that it never may*), and
so the deputation left the drawing-room.

How Blight managed to break this fresh sorrow to her
friend, and how she succeeded in supporting her through the
agony of that long sleepless night, are mysteries of kindness,
which we did not attempt to inquire into, but which have only
made us admire our poor persecuted governess the more, and
been the cause of our all *vowing never to teaze her, under any
pretence, again.*

*   *   *   *   *

The sun, darting into our little bedroom, awoke me very
early this morning, Nelly.   It was so happy and brilliant—as
brilliant as I should like to see it on my wedding day—that
I couldn't sleep.   I stole noiselessly along the corridor, and
peeped into Blight's chamber.   Mrs. Dove was asleep in her
bed, and Blight was lying outside, with her clothes on, asleep
also.   She had evidently fallen at last, with the fatigue of
watching.   The sun was shining brightly on them both.   On
the poor widow's face it fell as on a marble statue,—so deadly
pale, so immoveable were the features.   On the poor
governess's face, it alighted, as I thought, as on a sleeping
angel.   Her head was bathed in light, and around it I thought
the rays drew a golden line, that burned before my worshipping
eyes like a halo of glory.   I blessed her in the secrecy of my
soul, and, kneeling, kissed the hem of her garment.   There was
a slight noise—I tried to rise but couldn't—some strong power
kept me on my knees.   Blight awoke, and seeing me, pressed

me passionately to her breast, and wept, dear, wept like a mother over me. Oh, Nelly, may the purity of those tears, flowing from so good a woman, wash away all the stains out of my foolish heart, and turn all that is black in it as bright as the halo I saw this morning shining round her head !

She lifted me up, and carried me back to my room,—where, kissing me, she bade me not to say a word of what had passed. She then tucked me up in my little bed, and enjoining me tenderly " always to be a good girl," left me, with another kiss, long before any of the girls were awake.

   *   *   *   *

The ball has been postponed, as I have already told you, Nelly. What a change two short days have made in the school. One day we were full of hopes and schemes—our thoughts played with nothing but ribbons, and flowers, and flounces,—and the next our hopes, like all our voices, have been hushed, and the most boisterous expression of joy you can hear is a whisper. Only yesterday we were practising *Valses à Deux Temps* until we were tired, first of being the gentleman and then the lady, and now our footsteps, as we walk in twos-and-twos slowly up and down the room, sound with a hollow echo as if we were walking in a vault. Yesterday we were trying on each other's ear-rings and finery, and amusing ourselves with anticipations of Blight's ball-room dress, wondering where the drop of ink would be this time, and at present we are lost in admiration of her noble devotion to Mrs. Dove, and thinking that there is something finer in this world than fine clothes.

But, hush, here comes Mrs. Dove—so fearfully changed in so short a time—looking sad but resigned—a saint in suffering. She is leading by the hand her little boy. He is laughing and gambolling by her side,—unconscious of the pang each merry tone is sending to his mother's heart. Instantly upon her arrival the conversation ceases, as if we were entering a church, and all eyes and thoughts are turned to the poor

doomed martyr.   Blight advances to receive her, and the two
retire together into a quiet corner, and there, for the present,
Nelly, let us leave them.

I promise to tell you the remainder of this sad story in my
next.

Yours, my pretty Eleanor,

Very, very affectionately,

KITTY.

P.S. I have given a fourpenny piece (Amy lent it me) to
Mrs. Perkwisites (our charwoman), upon her promising me
most solemnly to drop this in the post.   I hope you'll receive
it, dear ?

This is a holiday, but, as you can imagine, not a very
joyful one.   The only interest is who can make the most of
baby on this his last day.

THE SEVENTEENTH LETTER LEFT.

(Dated Two Days before Breaking-up.)

SHOWING WHAT CRUELTIES PRIDE IS FREQUENTLY THE UNNATURAL PARENT OF.

THE day after I wrote to you, sweetest Nelly, I was
practising in the little drawing-room,—though my thoughts
were more upon the joy of the holidays that are so near than
upon the music that was before me,—when a magnificent
carriage drove up with two fat grey horses, and the roundest
cherub of a coachman I ever saw.   The panels were a perfect
picture, quite a nosegay of colours, and there were two
servants behind with liveries that tired your eyes as much as a
kitchen-fire !   You can fancy the sensation so grand a carriage
made outside our humble College.   All the windows were
instantly filled with staring faces, and there was scarcely a

house down the crescent but the cook and housemaid were
standing on the doorstep, having come out purposely to see what
was the matter.

This excitement was rather increased by such a " rat-tat-tat-
tat" (I think both footmen must have knocked at once) as
must have given the table-beer in the cellar a shaking that
would make it feel for several days still smaller.   The house
quite throbbed after it !   So great was the noise, that Susan had
thought it only respectful to put on her best cap, and there she
was standing in the hall, with a clean apron, waiting in a fever
of curiosity to know who were the grand visitors.

Presently, the beautiful heraldic door was thrown back, and,
after sundry tugs and pulls, out tumbled a gouty, puffy, white-
neck-clothed, old gentleman, shut up inside a perfect watch-
box of capes and great coats, of which the only window, or
door, was a small aperture left open in front of his red face.
All the rest of his body was locked up close by bars of braid
and endless bolts of buttons.   He was helped across the pave-
ment by a footman on each side, and I thought he never would
have finished the mere jump of a journey.   After him followed a
tall, thin, perpendicular, hop-pole of a lady, so stiff, dear, with
pride and Pompadour brocade, that it was a perfect wonder to
me how she contrived ever to sit down, and she walked into the
house with an air that plainly implied that Hammersmith
ought to be eternally indebted to her for having condescended
to visit its plebeian neighbourhood.   I am sure, Nelly, the poor
creatures seemed to undergo more trouble in getting out of
their carriage than most people would have felt in walking the
whole distance from town !

I was so engrossed with their movements — so lost in
admiration over the horses, and the prize coachman, and the
footmen with their rosy silk stockings, that I quite forgot they
were coming upstairs, and only remembered it when a short
wheezing noise told me it was too late to escape.   Nor (I am
ashamed to confess it) did I try much, when I heard the lady

say, with a voice every bit as proud as her walk, "*Tell Mrs.
Dove that Sir Alexander and Lady Dove are waiting to see
her.*" I ran into a little room at the back, that is meant to be
a conservatory, and hid myself behind some artificial plants.
I needn't tell you how frightened I was, for I *knew I was
doing wrong*, but still the strong interest I took in the poor
widow silenced the small voice of my conscience ; and if the
risk had been much greater, I really think I should have
braved it. I could observe everything that was going on without being seen myself. They looked a cross couple, with a
false air of plated gentility about them—nothing of the true
stamp which persons nobly born put upon wealth, but which
wealth never can put upon those who haven't the nobility either
of birth or soul in them. Theirs was clearly the pride of the
pocket—a pride that delights most in jingling its money and
insolence in the presence of the poor. Accordingly I felt for
Mrs. Dove ; for I could fancy the reception she was likely to
receive from such rich relations, who evidently were not much
in the habit of opening their hearts, unless it was done, as they
probably opened their purses, from a cold motive of ostentation.

She entered the room, ghastly pale, carrying her boy in her
arms, and scarcely able to reach the chair into which she
sank. Neither rose to receive her. Neither gave the poor
stricken woman one look of encouragement, one small word of
welcome.

There was an unpleasant pause, and the old gentleman
buried himself in a comfortable arm-chair, apparently quite
exhausted, and there he sat perfectly motionless, staring
vacantly before him, with the fine meditative expression I
have seen in the face of a turtle, to which his cold eye, and the
form of his bald head, bore no small resemblance ; the loose
folds of his handkerchief round his neck aiding singularly the
likeness. Then the stately lady, who seemed to relieve her
husband altogether of the fatigue of talking, broke the icy
silence. " We have received your note, Mrs. Dove, and attend

to-day to accept from your hands the child of our dear lost son, whose life, you must excuse me saying it, you cruelly sacrificed to your ambitious views. You know his marriage with you, which we possibly could not think of countenancing, was the cause of his leading the wild, disreputable life he did, and of its ending so fatally." (She stopped here, as if to recover from her maternal emotion, though I am sure she spoke as calmly as if she were engaging a servant, and then pompously continued.) "However, in receiving this dear charge, both Sir Alexander and myself are anxious to forget and forgive the irreparable injuries wrought by your unfeeling selfishness ; nay, you must pardon me if I am seemingly harsh, but I must speak the truth." (I should like to have flung a flower-pot at her head for doing it.) "To show further the kindly feeling that animates both Sir Alexander's bosom and my own, we have agreed to extend permission for your visiting the child (*her own child*, Nelly,) occasionally, but only after asking our previous sanction, which must be obtained through the application of your solicitor. It is exclusively upon this condition, and upon the clear understanding that you surrender all claim to the boy, that Sir Alexander and myself agree to adopt him, and to make him the inheritor of our joint wealth."

She waited, as though she expected applause to follow this grand speech, and, not taking any notice of her daughter-in-law's sobbing grief, coldly resumed :

"We are deeply pained, both Sir Alexander (he was nearly asleep, *in spite of his deep pain*) and myself, to hear of your ill-health, and to notice its too evident symptoms. As this interview must be equally distressing to both parties, you will oblige me, my dear madam, by immediately preparing the boy, and accepting our fond assurances that he shall receive every attention and love compatible with his new position from his second father and mother. It will be my greatest pride and pleasure to surround him with every happiness, so that he may never feel what it is to miss the loss of *you*, madam."

It was only after two or three efforts that Mrs. Dove could rise from the chair. She attempted to speak, but her voice failed her. She could only speak with her tears, and they could have but little effect in falling on the hearts they did. She bent her neck, as if to the cruelty of the decision, and, guiding herself by the wall, staggered out of the room.

How I longed for her to return. I did not like being left alone with these two unfeeling creatures, who had come to rob a mother of her child—trading upon her necessities to make an inhuman bargain with her. Their presence seemed to weigh upon the atmosphere. It gave me a sort of nightmare to look at them; I tried to run out of the room, but my limbs felt chained; I attempted to scream, but it was as much as I could do to breathe even. How I repented of my girlish curiosity! I was so unhappy I shouldn't have minded being found out—anything, so that some one had come into the room, and driven away the frightful oppressiveness of *being left alone* with that proud wicked man and woman!

To increase this discomfort, I was compelled to listen to their horrible conversation. Sir Alexander said but little : he seemed only to acquiesce, and his wife did all the talking. He was asked what he thought of "his fine daughter-in-law?"—whether he didn't think she was a " pretty weak thing "—" a delicate piece of goods "—" a nice fanciful lady's-maid for his son to marry ? " and he nodded assent to all these propositions. As a charitable finish, he was asked if he thought " she was long for this world ? " He did not break through the sustained wisdom of his silence, but simply exclaimed a round, fat, " Ah ! " which sounded exactly as if he was smacking his lips over a beautiful glass of port wine.

At last Mrs. Dove entered the room, and I breathed again. She seemed firmer than before. There was a determination in her manner—no timidity or hesitation in her steps. She was leading her boy by the hand. He was dressed in his little hat and coat, ready for the journey—a journey from which his mother might never see him return. She impressed one long, long despairing kiss upon his pretty lips, and then, shutting her eyes, placed him in Lady Dove's arms; this done she turned quickly away, and I could see her hands joined convulsively together, and her lips moving quickly, though I could not hear one word come from them.

Lady Dove received the boy—neither addressing nor noticing the poor mother, whose heart was bursting over the sacrifice. She was preparing without a word to leave the room, when the little fellow—beginning probably to awaken to the idea of being separated from his mother—set up a shrill scream of anger. Upon hearing the first sound of that beloved appeal, Mrs. Dove turned round, her head rose from the resting-place of her bosom, and her eyes flew with her thoughts to Heaven, whose aid she was invoking to carry her through this hard struggle. The boy still continued screaming. She was about to rush to him; but, no—she paused, and falling upon her knees, and *clasping her hands over her ears,* her body was soon bent in the full fervour of prayer.

I rushed out in a minute, and stood quietly by her side, not liking to disturb her holy meditations, but ready to offer any assistance she might need. There she remained long after the gorgeous carriage had carried away her darling. After a time she grew calmer; and when she turned round and noticed me, she fell upon my neck and, in a thrilling voice, which I shall never forget, so kind it was, though pierced through and through with tears, she *blessed me.*

Then, meekly as a child, she permitted me to lift her up, and to conduct her to Blight, who took her to her loving arms and nursed her, and did all that sympathy could do to stop the flow of grief that had been so deeply stabbed as hers.

Not a word did the poor afflicted one inquire about her boy! Blight says the only consolation that supports her in this severe trial is the knowledge that her child is provided for now for life.

I

The Lady Principal has given up her private rooms to the use of Mrs. Dove. I imagine she is secretly ashamed of her severity towards the poor governess, and wishes to make amends for it. She looks in every half-hour, asking if there is anything she can do, and has asked Blight to sit up with her friend all night, and they had better sleep in her room, and then *she* can keep Blight company. Ah! Nelly, I'm sure we should never commit an act of unkindness, if we could only foresee how sorry we should be for it afterwards!

I am called away, Nelly ; so, with the hastiest snatch of a kiss, good-bye.

Yours fondly and faithfully,

KITTY.

P.S. I shall see you now in two or three days, and then won't I give it you for not writing, you good-for-nothing, lazy thing!

P.S. Those tiresome examinations at last are over! I've got a prize for " *Calcul de Tête*," and a *carte de mérite* for my *Maintien*. The most curious thing is that St. Ledger, who is one of the dullest girls, and can hardly read the Marriage Service, has carried off five or six prizes! Meggy Sharpe says that it is all on account of the pine-apples, and pheasants, and jars of turtle and milk-punch which her papa is continually sending the Lady Principal. She says if she had been the daughter of an alderman, or if I had been in any way related to the *London Tavern*, that probably we should have been puffed into equal prodigies. This is too monstrous! and I cannot believe any schoolmistress would be guilty of such gross *favouritism*. However, it is a great wonder amongst us all how poor Plodder, who nearly turned her red hair grey by fagging, has not succeeded in gaining a single prize; but then Meggy says it would be folly to expect it, for her father is only a *small coal-merchant*, and that his daughter never will be clever until he has sense enough to send in *on trial* a waggon-load of his best coals. I don't believe a word of it.

I have done such a beautiful drawing—so beautiful that when our drawing-master showed it me, I did not recognise it as my own! How pleased papa and mamma will be! but I hope they will not ask me to draw when I am at home, or else I am afraid they will find out a sad difference between my scratchy efforts and the beautiful "Moonlight View of Tintern Abbey" (which is almost prettier, dear, than the drawings they hang in the shop windows where they sell pencils), that is at present lying before me with my name in the corner!

THE EIGHTEENTH LETTER LEFT.

(Dated " the last night at School.")

SHOWING THAT SCHOOL IS NOT SUCH A TERRIBLE PLACE AFTER ALL.

SUCH an event, Nelly! The School is in such an excitement, that, though I am to see you to-morrow, I cannot resist writing you a short account of it.

Yesterday evening, when we were all talking of the pleasure of returning home, and of the different pic-nics, theatres, balls and *fêtes* we expected to go to ; and were exchanging innumerable promises of visiting and inviting each other during the holidays ; a cab drove up to the door. In an instant we were all at the windows. Some ran to the door, and one or two contrived cleverly to be on the staircase at the very moment an elegant Lady was running up to the drawing-room. She enquired, in great anxiety, " for her niece ; " and, when asked who she meant, for she seemed to imagine, as a matter of course, that every one knew her niece, to our great astonishment we heard her say—" Why Fanny Dove, to be sure."

Immediately we all flew upstairs ; but to Blight was left the honour of conducting the poor invalid into the drawing-room. In the next minute—for the door had been left open, and we could see everything—she was locked in her aunt's arms, who was weeping over her brother's pride and treasure—scolding, caressing, cheering, and pitying, all in the same breath.

Then she asked after her little boy ; and, when Fanny, with blushes and trembling lips, had told the painful truth of his separation, the aunt cried still more, and angrily said—" For shame, Fanny—for shame, to part with your child ; but never mind, dear—come don't cry so—I will run into their house, if that's all, and carry him off myself ; and you shall never lose him again ; and the dear boy shall compensate with eternal love his angel mother for all the sacrifices she has made for his sake." Long before the finish of these endearments, the tone of anger, which at first had pierced the aunt's voice, had softened into tones of the most loving kindness ; and there she was, seated on the sofa by the side of Fanny, lavishing every tenderness she could think of in order to stop her tears. But, Nelly dear, they were tears, not of grief, or pain ; but tears of gratitude as pure as the heart from which they flowed. She smiled, and looked so beautiful, for I had never seen her smile before, and happiness played like so much sunshine about her face. It seemed as if the clouds, which so long had settled there, were clearing away, and that her soul was shining through her features, as it caught at last a bright glimpse of Heaven.

Shall I tell you of the touching farewell she took of the Lady Principal and the College, where she had known nothing but sorrow ? All recollection, however, of what she had endured had left her gentle breast, and she lingered now amongst us as if loth to part. We crowded round her, and I thought we never should get tired of shaking her by the hand, and kissing her, and wishing her all sorts of happiness.

At last, Aunt dragged her gently away. Resting on her

supporting arm, she followed as naturally as a child follows its
mother. As she was being led to the cab, the Aunt kept up a
continual soliloquy—as I have heard a nurse soothe an ailing
infant—singing by her side a murmuring lullaby of tenderness.
I heard her reproach her in this affectionate manner—"Ah!
you naughty, unkind Fanny, not to have sent earlier to your
poor Aunt. I suppose, you foolish girl, you were too proud?
and how could she know where you were; or that you were
dangerously ill?   However, never mind, dearest, we will make
up for lost time—you will soon get well in the country—and,
with your little boy, we shall feel so happy as if grief never
could touch us again, won't we, eh, my pretty lamb? you
dear, foolish, wicked Fanny, ever to have thought your aunt
loved you less than she really does."

With these soothing reproaches she was handed into the
cab. She looked out of the window to smile a last farewell,
when she perceived poor Blight, who was half-hiding behind
the hall-door. She sprang out in one minute, and, throwing
her arms round her neck, she ejaculated between her kisses and
her tears—"God bless you, my dearest friend, I hope I shall
never forget your kindness to me;" and a promise was
extorted from the Lady Principal that Blight was to pass the
holidays with them.

Fraulein Agatha told her most German stories that evening.
Mademoiselle tried to enliven us with some of her most
favourite anecdotes, that had never failed before to make us
laugh; but all in vain. Our thoughts would return to Fanny
Dove, and we could think and talk of nothing else.

My first half-year ends to-morrow. School does not appear
to me now the dreadful place—the awful Blue Beard's chamber
—that it did when first I peeped into it. I have learnt by
this time to respect my Schoolmistress. I know her sternness
is mostly assumed to frighten us into obedience; and, that
under her seeming severity there lurks a natural kindness that
would sooner at any period remit a punishment than inflict one.

Moreover, I can make allowances for her temper ever since I have had two little girls to look after myself; and have discovered how trying it is to put up with their thousand little provocations and to keep them out of mischief.   If it is difficult then with two girls—what must it be with sixty ?

But there is one thing, Nelly, which reconciles me to School more than any other, and which will always make me look back upon it with feelings of pleasure—I mean the good friends I have made since I have been here—friends, who I hope will continue to be my friends through life.

Besides, I have learnt one great truth, and that is to look with great respect, if not admiration, on many of our poor taskmasters and taskmistresses, who are tutoring and punishing themselves daily in the great school of adversity, all the time they are teaching us. What are our school-sufferings compared to theirs ?   What are their school-enjoyments in comparison with ours !

But, Nelly, I shall see you to-morrow; and there's no occasion to trouble you twice over with the same dreary common-places, which you will not care to laugh at, probably, more than once.   Till I see you, dearest, I remain.

Yours, most anxiously,

KITTY CLOVER.

P.S. Shall I ever be able to forgive you for not having answered my letters ?   But, probably, you have not had an opportunity of writing.

P.S. Tell dear Sydney I am coming home.   Has he forgotten me in six months ?   Whisper into his ear, I have a hair chain for him—*my own hair*—if he'll wear it.

P.S. There has been quite a rage for fainting lately. Every girl thought it her duty on the smallest pretext to faint.   However, Snapp threw a glass of vinegar over Noble's beautiful dove-coloured silk dress, and completely spoilt it. There has been no fainting since.

P.S. (*the last.*) *Her* husband came last night whistling and singing as usual. He thought to-night was to have been the grand ball. I am so glad he was disappointed. Blight told me (in confidence) he stopped very late, and was only persuaded at last to go upon being promised 100*l.* to go over to Australia and try his fortune there. Perhaps it's for the best ; but poor Mrs. Rodwell ! I'm ready to forgive her *all my fines and forfeits*, when I think of those that have been heartlessly levied upon *her.*

P.S. (*the very last.*) Oh dear ! Shan't I dream of Home to-night !

THIS WAS THE LAST LETTER LEFT AT THE PASTRYCOOK'S.

THE END.

LONDON:
BRADBURY AND EVANS, PRINTERS, WHITEFRIARS.